Whispers of Comfort: Sharing the Journey of Grief with Children, Teens, & Young Adults

By

Rhonda K. Gibb

Disclaimer:

The information provided in this book is for educational and informational purposes only. It is not intended as a substitute for professional advice or counseling. Readers are encouraged to seek the guidance of qualified professionals regarding any specific questions or concerns they may have about grief or supporting children, teens, or young adults through the grieving process. The author and publisher disclaim any liability arising from the use of information contained in this book.

About The Author:

Rhonda K. Gibb is not only a loving mother but also a caring champion for assisting children, teenagers, and young adults through the mourning process. With her history as an established content developer, she offers a unique combination of creativity and skill to her work. Drawing from her personal experiences as a parent and her knowledge of the obstacles young people encounter when dealing with loss, Rhonda has made it her mission to make grief easier for our younger generation.

Through her work, Rhonda delivers essential insights, practical direction, and emotional support to anyone navigating the road of bereavement. Her empathetic approach, along with her ability to portray complicated emotions in an accessible manner, connects powerfully with readers of all ages. Whether via emotional experiences, practical techniques, or artistic expressions, Rhonda's work inspires individuals to find healing, compassion, and hope despite loss.

As both a mother and a content producer, Rhonda knows the significance of promoting open communication, offering support, and establishing safe spaces for expressing emotions. Her devotion to helping young people navigate sorrow with resilience and strength shows through in her work, making her a valued resource for families, educators, and professionals alike. With Rhonda K. Gibb's leadership, grief may become a path of development, knowledge, and finally, healing for our younger generation.

Table of Contents

Introduction:

Smiling Through Grief: A Guide for Children, Teens, and Young Adults

Have you ever felt a sadness so deep it seemed like a wave, crashing over you and pulling you under? Maybe it happened when a beloved pet crossed the rainbow bridge, or perhaps a dear grandparent whispered their last goodbye. Maybe, just maybe, it was someone even closer, leaving a hollowness you didn't know existed. This feeling, dear reader, is called grief, and it's a journey we all take at some point in life.

It doesn't matter how old you are or how much your heart hurts; Whispers of Comfort will be there to accompany you on that path. Whether you're a little child just starting to explore the world, an energetic adolescent dealing with complicated emotions, or a young adult adjusting to this new reality, you'll find comfort and encouragement in these pages.

Imagine this book as a comforting embrace, a place where you may unwind and sort out all the mixed feelings you're experiencing. We'll talk about the sadness that washes over you like a storm, the fury that could swell up like a volcano, and even the confusion that swirls like a lost butterfly. We'll realize that everyone grieves differently, just like snowflakes are no two alike, and that's okay.

We will discover healthy methods to express ourselves together as we make memories, tell stories, and share tales. Our conversation will center on lovingly remembering, reaching out to loved ones for assistance, and finding inner strength and resilience.

This trip may not be easy, but you don't have to do it alone. Whispers of Comfort is here to hold your hand, share your tears, and celebrate your laughter, reminding you that even in the darkest night, stars still shine. So, take a deep breath, dear reader, and flip the page. This trip begins today, and together, we'll find our way to the light.

Remember, you are braver than you believe, stronger than you seem, and loved more than you realize.

The world might feel terribly huge and complicated when grief comes over you, like a tidal wave robbing your breath and leaving you dizzy on the shore. That's okay, it occurs to everyone. Whether you're a little one who feels adrift without your energetic dog, a teenager attempting to grasp the abrupt silence where your grandparent's laughter used to be, or a young adult facing the new landscape of losing a good friend, you're not alone in this storm. Whispers of Comfort is a life raft, here to steady you through the waves and take you into calmer waters.

Think of this book as a pleasant fire on a winter night, crackling with understanding and warmth. We'll congregate around its glow, sharing stories like stars in the sky. You'll learn that the tears you cry are like cleaning rain, fertilizing the seeds of love and remembrance you carry within. The rage that rises up, hot and blazing, is simply your heart screaming its truth. And the confusion? Ah, that's simply your mind attempting to make sense of what happened, and that's entirely natural.

Remember that little dandelion fluff, borne by the wind? Every one of us grieves differently, just like those fluffy seeds go in individual paths. Some might settle immediately, close to the source, while others dance on the breeze for miles before finding their resting place. There's no right or wrong way to grieve, no competition in who reveals their pain the loudest or hides it the best. We'll explore all the varied shades of mourning, from the profound blues of sorrow to the startling bursts of laughter that sometimes peek through the clouds.

But you won't just be exploring alone. We'll create memories together, like brilliant mosaics stitching together the lovely life of the one you mourn. We'll write letters filled with love and laughter, plant a tree in their honor, or make their favorite cookies, sharing the stories that keep their memory alive.

And when the path seems overwhelming, know you're surrounded by a lighthouse of support. We'll discuss reaching out to family and friends who can offer a warm hug and a listening ear. We'll explore the prospect of joining a support group, where you might find consolation amongst others who understand your experience. Remember, even the mightiest oak started as a little acorn, needing encouragement to grow strong.

This journey of mourning may not be paved with brightness, but Whispers of Comfort will be your steadfast companion. We'll walk with you hand-in-hand, reminding you that even in the darkest night, the stars still shine. You'll discover a strength you never knew you had, a resilience that blooms even through tears.

So, take a deep breath, dear reader, open this book, and let's go on this journey together. You are braver than you imagine, stronger than you seem, and loved more than you realize. And within these pages, you'll discover the whispers of comfort to remind you of that reality, every step of the way.

Within these pages, you'll find:

Gentle words of understanding: Like a loving embrace, these words will acknowledge your pain and affirm your emotions. You'll find comfort in knowing you're not alone on this road.

Creative exercises and prompts: From writing letters to creating a memory garden, these activities will help you express your thoughts in a healthy and meaningful way.

Real-life tales and realistic examples: You'll connect with the experiences of those who have walked similar pathways, finding peace and inspiration in their journeys.

Tips and tactics for coping with grief: Discover practical skills to manage unpleasant emotions, navigate challenging situations, and find moments of serenity despite the storm.

A helpful community: Feel the warmth of understanding and know that you're surrounded by people who care. This book will connect you to resources and support groups where you may share your experiences and find strength in numbers.

Remember, healing takes time, and there's no right or wrong way to grieve. This book is here to walk beside you, providing a safe environment to explore your emotions, find solace, and uncover your inner power. So, turn the page, my reader, and let's go on this voyage together. You are braver than you imagine, stronger than you seem, and loved more than you realize.

PART ONE:

Understanding Grief: The Rollercoaster of Feelings

Imagine your heart like a boat, cruising gently across a quiet ocean. Suddenly, a storm hits. Waves crash, the wind howls, and you feel terrified, puzzled, maybe even a little angry. That's kind of what grief feels like. It's a natural reaction to losing someone or something important, like a beloved pet, a close friend, or even a dream you had.

But unlike a storm that passes fast, grieving can feel like a rollercoaster. Sometimes you could feel sad, like your boat is tossed by big waves. Other times, you might be angry, like the wind is whipping your face. There might even be periods of perplexity, where the fog sweeps in and you don't know which direction to turn.

The essential thing to remember is that all these emotions are okay. It's normal to feel sad, angry, bewildered, afraid, or even relieved following a loss. Just like a rollercoaster has its ups and downs, sadness takes you on a trip of diverse feelings.

What Precisely is Grief?

Grief is your body and mind's method of saying goodbye. It's a process of healing, like repairing a broken bone. It takes time, and there's no one-size-fits-all solution. Just like everyone rides a rollercoaster differently, some people could cry a lot, while others might go quiet. Some might find solace in talking about their feelings, while others might prefer to express themselves through art, music, or writing.

Here are some things to remember regarding grief:

It's okay to be sad. Don't bottle up your emotions. Crying is a good way to release sadness.

It's alright to be angry. Sometimes, when we feel upset, rage might surge up. It's good to express your anger in a safe way, like striking a pillow or journaling.

It's acceptable to be perplexed. You might not understand why you're feeling the way you're feeling. That's okay! It takes time to process a loss.

You're not alone. Lots of individuals suffer grief, and there are people who care about you and want to assist. Talk to your parents, friends, instructors, or even a therapist if you need help.

Remember, you're powerful and capable of healing. The rollercoaster ride of grief could feel dangerous, but it's crucial to hold on tight and know that you're not alone. With time, love, and support, you'll make your way back to calm seas, bringing the memory of your loved one with you.

Life throws us many curveballs, and the loss of a loved one is surely one of the most profound and challenging. Grief, the emotional response to great loss, comes over us in waves, unpredictable and often overpowering.

Part One of this voyage takes you by the hand and guides you through the early phases of comprehending and navigating this complex storm.

Chapter 1: The Journey Begins provides the foundation, gently introducing the notion of sorrow and validating the numerous feelings that arise. This beginning chapter combines familiar analogies and avoids scientific jargon, offering a secure and inviting space for you to realize your unique experience. You'll find yourself nodding along as the writing normalizes the rollercoaster of feelings you may be experiencing, telling you that you're not alone on this trip.

Chapter 2: Waves of Feelings explores further into the emotional terrain of grief. It explores the variety of feelings you could encounter, from the crushing weight of melancholy and the sting of rage to the dizzying fog of disorientation. This chapter also educates you with healthy coping methods to negotiate these powerful emotions constructively, helping you find moments of peace amidst the turbulence.

Chapter 3: Everyone Grieves Differently celebrates the individuality of mourning. It emphasizes that there's no right or wrong way to grieve, and that your own expression of loss is valid and cherished. This chapter encourages you to accept your individual journey, reminding you that everyone recovers at their own rate and through their own routes.

By going on this trip, you'll receive essential insights into the nature of sorrow, learn to cope with the emotional waves it brings, and find peace in knowing that you're not alone on this route. Remember, sorrow is a process, not a destination. Part One serves as your anchor, offering empathy, support, and guidance as you negotiate the beginning phases of this transforming journey.

Chapter 1:

The Journey Begins: Embracing the Rainbow After the Rain

Have you ever built a sandcastle on the beach, only to see it washed away by a quick wave? The disappointment might seem like a hit in the gut, leaving you perplexed, maybe even a bit enraged. That's kind of how grieving feels sometimes. It's the sad, perplexing, and often even furious emotion when someone or something we love goes, like a beloved toy becoming misplaced or a favorite pet crossing the rainbow bridge.

Think of grief as a storm. Sometimes it's a light drizzle, making you feel a bit sad. Other times, it's a roaring cyclone, hurling you about with intense feelings like despair, rage, and uncertainty. It could feel dangerous and overpowering, but remember, storms always pass, and so will this emotional rollercoaster. Just like snowflakes, everyone's pain is unique. Some people could cry a lot, while others might become silent and aloof. Some might feel like talking about it, while others could express their sentiments via sketching, music, or writing.

There's no right or wrong way to feel, and it's good to experience a broad range of emotions.

This chapter is like your raincoat and umbrella for this storm. We'll explore what sorrow is, why it happens, and most importantly, how to manage its waves with courage and understanding. We'll utilize easy-to-understand language and real examples, so you never feel lost in the rain.

1. What is Grief?

Think of grieving as a journey, a way our hearts and brains recover after losing someone or something we love. It's not a monster under the bed, but a natural tide of emotions flowing over us. It's like the ocean after a hurricane — sometimes it's tumultuous and wild, other times it's beautiful and serene.

Understanding Grief: A Journey Through the Waves
Grief. The term itself might inspire sentiments of grief, bewilderment, and even terror. But what precisely is grief? While it typically comes accompanied by deep feelings, it's more than just melancholy. It's a complicated path our

emotions and minds undergo to recover after losing something really treasured.

Think about it like this: Imagine your life as a tranquil, blue ocean. Suddenly, a storm comes, forcing waves to smash and the water to churn. This storm indicates a loss, be it the passing of a loved one, the end of a relationship, or even the loss of a dream. The churning water? That's grief.

The Waves of Grief:
Just like a storm doesn't stay the same, sorrow unfolds in many forms and intensities. Sometimes, it's a huge surge of despair, smashing over you and leaving you gasping for air. Tears flow easily, and the sensation of emptiness may be overwhelming. But other times, sadness could be a subtle river, a continual undertow pushing you beneath the surface of your typical feelings. You can feel numb, puzzled, or simply "off."

It's crucial to remember that these waves, whether great or tiny, are all part of the trip. They're your body and mind's natural response to processing the loss and attempting to create a new normal.

The beauty of the ocean comparison resides in the reality that storms don't stay forever. After the waves subside, the water slowly settles, reflecting the beautiful blue sky once more. This doesn't imply the loss evaporates, but it signals that healing is possible.

The path of mourning could feel lengthy and grueling, but with time and support, you'll start to find moments of serenity within the waves. You'll learn to carry the memory of your loss with love and acceptance, finding new ways to navigate life's currents.

Note:
There's no right or wrong way to grieve. Everyone's path is unique.

Your sentiments are valid. Don't bottle things up — express them in healthy ways.

Healing takes time. Be gentle with yourself and realize that you're not alone.

Seek help. Talk to loved ones, join a support group, or seek professional treatment.

Grief may be a storm, but it doesn't have to drown you. Embrace the voyage, ride the waves with confidence, and know that there's a calm, brighter sea waiting on the other side.

Remember, the ocean always finds its way back to serenity, and so will you.
Understanding sorrow as a voyage through waves is a strong comparison, but let's go further into the subtleties of this complicated emotion.

The Many Faces of Grief:
While sadness is frequently the first feeling connected with loss, it's simply one facet of this complex diamond. Grief may emerge in a number of ways, depending on the individual and the nature of the loss:

Anger: Sometimes, the grief of loss transforms into anger against the person we lost, the situation, or even ourselves. It's vital to accept this rage and express it appropriately, not repress it.

Panic: The uncertain future following a loss can be unsettling, leading to worry and panic. Talking about your anxieties with loved ones or a therapist might help you negotiate this uncertainty.

Guilt: "Could I have done something different?" This question typically haunts people mourning, leading to guilt. Remember, you did the best you could with the knowledge and conditions you had.

Numbness: Sometimes, the agony of loss is so intense that we distance ourselves emotionally, feeling numb and disconnected. This is a coping technique, but be aware of it and seek assistance if it persists.

Acceptance: The ultimate purpose of the mourning process is not to forget, but to learn to live with the loss and discover acceptance. This doesn't imply condoning what happened, but accepting it and moving ahead with love in your heart.

The Uniqueness of Each Journey:
Remember, sorrow is not a one-size-fits-all experience. Your experience will be diverse from others' based on your personality, the nature of your loss, and your support system. Comparing your experience to others might be destructive - appreciate your own unique route.

Just as the ocean floor is variegated, so too is the terrain of healing. Some find peace in artistic expression like writing or painting, while others seek comfort in nature or spending time with loved ones. There's no right or wrong method to heal — find what resonates with you.

Navigating the waves of sorrow can be tough, but you don't have to do it alone. Seek help from family, friends, therapists, or support groups. Talking to others who understand your grief may be immensely affirming and beneficial.

Grief doesn't diminish the love you shared with the person or object you lost. Carry those wonderful memories with you, enabling them to offer comfort and courage throughout challenging times.

Beyond the Storm:
Remember, the storm doesn't define the ocean. Just as the light ultimately bursts through the clouds, so too will you rise from the depths of sadness. It may take time, but with patience, self-compassion, and support, you will find your way back to calmer seas, carrying the lessons learned and the love treasured inside your heart.

This journey is about examining the multiple faces of loss, respecting its uniqueness, finding your route to healing, and remembering with love. You are strong, you are competent, and you are not alone. Dive into the ocean of sadness with bravery, and know that the calm awaits you on the other side.

2. Feeling Different is Okay!

Just like every wave in the ocean is distinct, our sadness is individual too. Some individuals could cry like raindrops, while others might feel silent and aloof like a buried reef. Some could even feel angry like a crashing wave, and that's entirely alright! There's no right or incorrect way to feel amid a storm.

Imagine a box packed with bright bits of glass, each one reflecting a distinct color of light. This box signifies grief, and each unique component within depicts the varied ways individuals feel it. There's no single color that describes the complete scene - just like there's no single way to cry.

The Spectrum of Emotions:
Instead of a single wave slamming down, think of sorrow as a kaleidoscope, showing a vivid array of emotions:

Tears like Raindrops: Some express loss via open tears, allowing their anguish to flow freely. This is a good approach to release emotion and achieve catharsis.

Stillness like a Reef: Others could internalize their loss, looking quieter and more distant. This introspective approach lets people process their feelings at their own time.

Anger like a Crashing Wave: Some persons experience the pain of loss via anger, irritation, or even bitterness. Recognizing and expressing this anger in healthy ways helps people move on.

Confusion like a Murky Tide: The suddenness of loss might leave individuals feeling bewildered and puzzled. This is a typical reaction, and seeking understanding and support can help explain their emotions.

Laughter like Sparkling Sunlight: Though apparently contradictory, periods of joy and laughter may coexist alongside pain. Remembering joyful memories and clinging onto loved times may be a source of strength and consolation.

Just like each ray of light refracts differently through the glass, your experience of loss is uniquely yours. Don't compare your path to others — their showers won't destroy your tranquil power, and their thundering waves won't reduce your serene reflection. Embrace your particular expression of loss, recognizing there's no right or wrong way to grieve.

Pay attention to your emotions and how they appear. Do you find relief in talking it out with friends? Does journaling your feelings provide you comfort? Perhaps expressing oneself via art or spending time in nature resonates with you. There's no one-size-fits-all strategy to coping, so explore multiple possibilities and find what provides you consolation and understanding.

Accepting that your sorrow will likely be expressed in many and perhaps apparently conflicting ways is vital. Acknowledge your feelings, allow yourself to feel them without judgment, and seek assistance when required. Remember, the kaleidoscope of mourning is not static — the colors will move and alter over time, and that's absolutely acceptable.

Just like the varied colors in a kaleidoscope form a beautiful display, the different expressions of sadness present a profound portrait of our shared humanity. Recognizing and honoring the distinctiveness of each person's experience creates compassion and understanding.

Remember, the storm of loss may bring a combination of feelings, but you are not alone. Each component in your own kaleidoscope carries worth, and together they make a beautiful and unique representation of your path. Embrace the hues, navigate the storm, and remember, there's always a rainbow waiting on the other side.

3. Understanding Your Inner Storm

Grief, like the ocean, can be a huge and unpredictable force. While melancholy is frequently the most known emotion connected with loss, it's simply the tip of the iceberg. To really traverse this difficult path, we need to go further into the gamut of emotions that may develop, recognizing not just their presence, but also their purpose and appropriate strategies to handle them.

1. Sadness: The Heavy Anchor:
This is the most known face of sadness, a
profound and persistent sensation of sorrow,
emptiness, and desire. It may emerge as tears, a
lack of motivation, or a retreat from social
engagement. Sadness acts as a reminder of the
loss, a required acknowledgment of the grief.
Allow yourself to experience it, express it via
tears, journaling, or creative outlets, but
remember, sorrow doesn't have to define you.

2. Anger: The Roaring Storm:
Sometimes, the agony of loss changes into a
fierce wrath. You could feel bitter towards the
person or event that caused the loss, furious with
yourself, or even the world itself. This fury is a
natural reaction to feeling helpless and hurt.
Acknowledge it, express it in healthy ways like
exercise, writing, or talking to someone you
trust, but don't let it overtake you.

3. Confusion: The Foggy Mist:
Loss may leave you feeling bewildered and adrift,
like a ship without a compass. You could doubt
all you thought you understood, and the future
can appear murky and unclear. This uncertainty
is a natural aspect of digesting the unexpected.
Seek clarity by talking to loved ones, seeking

expert help, or simply allowing yourself time to grasp your evolving feelings.

4. Fear: The Treacherous Undertow:
The uncertain future following loss can be daunting, producing feelings of worry and anxiety. You can worry about your ability to cope, the influence on your life, or the likelihood of more losses. This worry is valid, but remember, you're not alone. Talk to someone you trust, try relaxation methods, and focus on the present moment, where you have the power to navigate.

5. Guilt: The Whispering Shadow:
"Could I have done something different?" This question can torment individuals' mourning, leading to feelings of shame and self-blame. Remember, you did the best you could with the facts and conditions you had at the time. Forgive yourself, let go of the "what-ifs," and focus on learning and moving forward with love.

Note:
These are just some of the numerous feelings you could face on your grieving journey.

It's totally common to experience a combination of them all, sometimes even simultaneously.

There's no right or wrong way to feel. Don't evaluate yourself or compare your experience to others.

Seek help from loved ones, therapists, or support groups. Talking about your feelings may be immensely affirming and beneficial.

Each emotion has a function, helping you process the loss and recover. Acknowledge them, express them properly, and move through them with care for yourself.

Remember, the storm may be roaring now, but just like the water ultimately settles, so will your emotions. With understanding, self-compassion, and support, you'll learn to manage the waves and make your way back to calmer seas, carrying the lessons learned and the love treasured inside your heart.

This chapter is just the beginning of your mourning journey. In the following chapter, we'll explore these emotions in greater detail and uncover appropriate strategies to manage them. We'll also discover how everyone grieves differently and how to honor your own route through this storm.

Remember, even if the journey might seem tough right now, the sun will ultimately shine again, and you'll discover calmer seas. You're strong, capable, and loved, and you have the power to manage this storm and find healing.

Bonus Tip: Throughout your journey, think of this book as your lighthouse, leading you through the darkness and helping you find your way back to the light.

Chapter 2:

Waves of Feelings: Exploring and Navigating Grief's Emotional Seas

Grief, like the ocean, is a huge and powerful force. It gives you waves of emotions, some soft and some crashing, all bringing you on a road of healing after loss. This chapter addresses the many emotions connected with loss, concentrating on sadness, anger, and confusion, and offers you with healthy coping skills to traverse these waves effectively.

1. Unveiling the Depths of Sadness:

Sadness, the ever-present shadow of sadness, casts a lengthy and complex shadow on our emotions. Understanding its subtleties and navigating its depths are essential steps in recovery. Let's go further into this emotion:

Understanding the Layers of Sadness:
The Physical Ache: The aching in your chest, the tightness in your throat, the weight in your limbs — these are all physical signs of emotional suffering. Acknowledge them, listen to what your body is telling you.

The Overwhelming Loss: The absence cries loud. Whether it's the vacant chair, the quiet laughter, or the unrealized goals, the continual reminder of what's gone may be stifling. Allow yourself to grieve the exact intricacies, the unique fabric of your relationship with the lost one.

The Constant Yearning: Memories dance like fireflies in your memory, leaving behind a path of desire. You hunger for their touch, their voice, their presence. Acknowledge this need, but remember, it's fuelled by love, not a wish to stay in the past.

The Tears: Don't hold them back. Tears are a natural cleaning process, a method to discharge the pent-up emotions. Cry in alone or with loved ones, let the tears fall freely, and trust their healing power.

The Gray Haze: The world loses its vitality, colors become subdued, and joy feels like a distant memory. This is a typical response to emotional upheaval. Be patient, allow yourself to enjoy this time without judgment.

Healthy Ways to Cope with Sadness:
Journaling: Pour your heart onto paper, express your feelings without filters, and observe them

take shape on the page. This process of externalizing your feelings may be immensely relieving.

Creative Expression: Let your melancholy flow through art, music, poetry, or any kind of creative expression that connects with you. Creativity enables for emotional processing and might provide unexpected consolation.

Nature's Embrace: Immerse yourself in the splendor of nature. Take walks in the park, listen to the ocean waves, or simply sit beneath a tree and breathe deeply. Nature has a soothing and rejuvenating influence on the psyche.

Reminiscing: Share joyful memories with loved ones, look at old pictures, or revisit locations you treasured together. While it may cause tears, remembering also celebrates the life that was and keeps the link alive.

Support Groups: Connect with people who understand your hardship. Sharing your stories and finding peace in shared loss may be immensely powerful.

Therapy: Seeking professional therapy can give useful tools and coping methods for managing your pain and navigating the intricacies of grieving.

Remember:
Sadness is not a weakness: It's a natural and healthy emotion to loss. Don't criticize yourself for experiencing it.
There's no schedule for healing: Grief unfolds at its own rate. Be patient with yourself and allow the process to take its course.
grief doesn't have to overtake you: While it may feel overpowering at times, remember that pleasure and thankfulness may coexist with grief. Find moments of light and grasp onto them.

You are not alone: Reach out for assistance, share your burden, and realize that there is love and understanding ready to welcome you.

By completely grasping the depths of sadness and embracing healthy coping techniques, you may begin to traverse its waves and emerge stronger on the other side. Remember, you are not alone on this path.

2. Navigating the Storm of Anger:

Anger, an often-surprising yet immensely frequent emotion in mourning, can feel like a turbulent storm within. It's crucial to understand its foundations, negotiate its intensity, and discover healthy methods to express it without causing harm to yourself or others. Let's explore further into this complicated emotion:

Unveiling the Layers of Anger:
The Sting of Injustice: Grief frequently produces thoughts of unfairness, a questioning of "why them?" This sense of unfairness can inspire anger directed outwardly, at fate, at the world, or even at medical experts. Acknowledge this anger, understand its cause, and attempt to reframe it as a reflection of your profound love and the desire for a different outcome.

Frustration and Powerlessness: In the face of loss, we frequently feel powerless to change the situation. This impotence might emerge as irritation, either inside at ourselves for not being able to "save" them, or outside at those who seem unaffected. Recognize this irritation as an indication of your great yearning to protect and care for the lost one.

Underlying Hurt and Fear: Anger typically hides deeper feelings like grief, anguish, and fear. The rage could be a protective strategy, a means to avoid addressing the vulnerability and raw feelings underlying. Explore what lies underlying the anger, allow yourself to feel those feelings, and express them in healthy ways.

Blaming Yourself or Others: Sometimes, rage takes the shape of self-blame ("I could have done more") or blame towards others ("It's their fault they're gone"). While it's natural to question and look for explanations, realize that blaming rarely gives peace. Practice self-compassion and accept that no one is to fault for the loss.

Healthy Ways to Channel Anger in Grief:
Physical Activity: Exercise may be a strong outlet for releasing pent-up rage. Go for a run, go to the gym, or participate in any physical exercise that helps you to move your body and release the emotional energy.

Creative Expression: Channel your anger into art, music, writing, or any creative medium that resonates with you. Expressing your anger creatively may be cathartic and give a healthy channel for its release.

Assertiveness Training: Learn better methods to express your anger assertively, creating boundaries and conveying your demands without resorting to confrontation or blaming. This may be immensely useful in handling uncomfortable talks and circumstances.

Journaling: Write down your furious thoughts and feelings without judgment. This can help you analyze them, identify their origins, and find better methods to express them.

Talking to a Therapist: Professional help may give a safe environment to explore your anger, unravel its underlying feelings, and create healthy coping methods for managing it effectively.

Important Reminders:
Expressing anger doesn't mean acting on it: It's vital to discern between expressing your anger and letting it dictate your behavior. Find healthy channels for expression that don't hurt yourself or others.

Anger is part of the mourning process: Don't criticize yourself for feeling furious. It's a valid and natural response to loss. Allow yourself to experience it, but don't let it dominate you.

Seek assistance: If your anger becomes overpowering or leads to unhealthy actions, contact out for professional support. A therapist can help you understand your anger and build appropriate coping methods.

Focus on healing: Remember that the ultimate objective is to heal. While anger may be a part of the trip, don't allow it get in the way of your general well-being.

By recognizing the layers of fury in mourning and finding appropriate methods to express it, you can weather the storm and emerge stronger on the other side. Remember, you are not alone on this path.

3. Deciphering the Fog of Uncertainty:

Grief isn't only about grief and anger; it may also leave you wrapped in a dense fog of uncertainty, disorientation, and a questioning of your very identity. This inner conflict, while disconcerting, is a typical component of processing grief. Let's go further into this baffling time and examine strategies to discover clarity within the haze:

Understanding the Layers of Confusion:
Lost Identity: When a loved one is gone, a part of your own identity is lost with them. Roles change, habits vary, and the comfortable footing you stood on seems to vanish. Acknowledge this sensation of identity loss and allow yourself to explore who you are becoming in this new world.

Questioning Purpose: The future you envisioned might feel fuzzy and unclear. You can doubt your life's purpose, job direction, or even the meaning of existence itself. This is a natural reaction to the interruption of your life plan. Give yourself time to investigate these topics without pressure to find fast solutions.

Reality Distorted: Grief can distort your perspective of reality. Memories could feel blurry, dreams vivid, and the sense of time confused. Acknowledge these alterations and remind yourself that your perspective is changing to the new realities of your existence.

Emotional Rollercoaster: The cloud of bewilderment typically comes with a tornado of emotions: grief, rage, fear, guilt, and more. These feelings might conflict and leave you feeling overwhelmed and confused of how to react. Recognize them as valid responses and allow yourself to feel them without judgment.

Finding Clarity in the Haze:
Mindfulness Practices: Techniques like meditation, deep breathing, and mindful movement can help anchor you in the present moment and minimize the sense of being overwhelmed by confusion. Focus on your breath, your environment, and the feelings in your body to center yourself.

Journaling: Expressing your ideas and feelings, even if they appear confused, can provide clarity and insight. Don't restrain yourself; simply write out whatever comes to mind. You could uncover trends, feelings, or questions you weren't aware of previously.

Routine and Structure: Amidst the commotion, creating a routine may bring a feeling of regularity and stability. Stick to regular sleep and mealtimes, even if it feels tough. Engaging in familiar hobbies may also bring a sense of comfort and grounding.

Open Communication: Talk to trustworthy friends, family members, or a therapist about your confusion. Sharing your story might ease feelings of loneliness and give other views to assist you navigate the fog.

Patience and Self-Compassion: Remember, mending takes time. Don't expect to have all the answers quickly. Treat yourself with care and tolerance, realizing that this disorientation is a brief phase in your mourning journey.

Important Reminders:
Confusion is not weakness: It's a natural and healthy reaction to a severe loss. Don't condemn yourself for feeling lost or uncertain.

This too shall pass: The fog of confusion may feel thick and impenetrable right now, but remember, it will eventually lift. With time and self-compassion, you will find your way through it.

Seek assistance: Talking to a therapist or joining a grieving support group may give essential support and advice as you negotiate the intricacies of sorrow and bewilderment.

By recognizing the layers of uncertainty and embracing useful coping methods, you may begin to discover clarity and emerge from the fog stronger and more resilient. Remember, you are not alone on this path.

4. Understanding and Navigating the Shadows of Fear

Fear, while frequently unsaid, may be a powerful and persistent factor in sorrow. It sneaks in with grief, anger, and uncertainty, changing our sense of loss in fundamental ways. Let's go deeper into understanding and coping with this complicated emotion:

Understanding Fear's Many Faces:
Fear of the Unknown: Loss takes us into uncertain land. We worry about the future without our loved one, the changes it will bring, and the obstacles we'll confront. This dread might show as anxiety, concern, and a sense of powerlessness.

Fear of Abandonment: Grief exposes our vulnerability and the fragility of existence. We can fear more losses, loneliness, and isolation, especially if our loved one offered emotional support or stability. This anxiety might lead to clinginess, disengagement, or difficulties developing new bonds.

Worry of Failure: We could worry about not respecting the memory of our loved one, failing to move on, or forgetting them. This anxiety might emerge as perfectionism, remorse, or unwillingness to let go of old patterns.

Fear of Death: Our own mortality becomes brutally obvious after a loss. We could fear our own death, the agony it will inflict on loved ones, or the unknown beyond this life. This anxiety might lead to existential inquiries, avoidance of reminders of death, or clinging to the present.

Coping with Fear in a Healthy Way: Acknowledge and Accept: Don't suppress your fear. Acknowledge its presence and embrace grief as a valid response to your loss. Ignoring it will just make it grow stronger.

Talk It Out: Share your anxieties with trustworthy friends, family, or a therapist. Talking about them helps alleviate their load and give other perspectives.

Seek Comforting Rituals: Establish routines that provide you comfort and a sense of control, such visiting your loved one's cemetery, lighting a candle, or engaging in activities they enjoyed.

Mindfulness and Relaxation Techniques: Practices like meditation, deep breathing, and progressive muscle relaxation can help manage anxiety and panic by anchoring you in the present moment.

Focus on Small Steps: Don't strive to overcome all your worries at once. Set tiny, realistic objectives and celebrate each step forward, no matter how little.

Seek Professional Help: If your fear is overpowering or is interfering with your everyday life, don't hesitate to seek professional treatment from a therapist or counselor specialized in mourning.

Important Reminders:
Fear is normal: Many individuals sense terror amid mourning. You are not alone in feeling this way.

Fear doesn't have to control you: With knowledge and good coping techniques, you may control your fear and move ahead on your recovery path.

Self-compassion is key: Be gentle to yourself. Give yourself time and space to recover at your own pace.

Focus on hope: While dread may be present, realize that there is still hope for the future. You may discover fresh purpose and delight in life, even after loss.

By recognizing the varied types of dread in mourning and adopting healthy coping techniques, you may begin to traverse its shadows and emerge stronger and more resilient. Remember, you are not alone on this path. There is aid and support available, and you have the strength to conquer your worries and achieve healing.

5. Guilt in Grief: Untangling the Knot of Self-Blame

Grief's heavy heart frequently bears an additional burden: shame. This complicated feeling may wrap itself around our memories, generating a stifling sense of obligation and blame. Let's study the numerous faces of guilt in sorrow and how to cope with them:

Understanding Guilt's Many Facets:
Regretful Actions: This guilt originates from specific words or acts, real or imagined, that we feel contributed to the death or caused agony to our loved one. It might emerge as persistent

thoughts, replaying experiences, and hoping for "if onlys."

Inaction and Missed Opportunities: We may feel guilty for something we didn't do, including failing to show our love adequately, not seeking medical alternatives enough, or squandering quality time. This remorse frequently focuses on the "what ifs" and squandered chances.

Survivor's Guilt: When surrounded by loss, a nagging sense of guilt might grow for still being alive. This apparently inexplicable sensation is a complex combination of relief, grief, and asking why you were saved but your loved one wasn't.

Societal Expectations: Societal pressures and implicit expectations can generate guilt. Comparing oneself to others, feeling judged, or internalizing societal standards about sorrow can make us feel like we're "not grieving right" and lead to self-blame.

Coping with Guilt in a Healthy Way:
Challenge Your Thoughts: Guilt generally rests on erroneous thinking habits. Identify these tendencies, assess the data rationally, and replace them with self-compassionate beliefs.

Ask yourself: "Would I blame someone else the same way?"

Seek Forgiveness: Forgive yourself, not to erase the loss but to embrace your humanity and let go of self-punishment. Remember, you couldn't control everything, and your intentions were likely good.

Focus on What You Can Do: Instead of obsessing on the past, put your energy into efforts that respect your loved one's memory, contribute to their legacy, or just provide you comfort.

Connect with Others: Talk about your guilt with trusted friends, relatives, or a therapist. Sharing your load might alleviate its weight and bring other perspectives.

Practice Self-Care: Guilt may deplete your vitality, making it important to prioritize self-care. Engage in things that feed your body and spirit, including exercise, relaxation methods, or spending time in nature.

Seek Professional Help: If guilt becomes overpowering or interferes with your everyday life, don't hesitate to seek professional treatment from a therapist specialized in grieving and guilt.

Important Reminders:
Guilt is not a measure of your love: Feeling sorry doesn't imply you loved your lost one less. It's a normal response to a difficult issue.

You are not alone: Guilt is quite frequent with mourning. Many individuals feel it, and you don't have to go through it alone.
Forgiveness is possible: You can forgive yourself, even if others haven't. It's a path of self-compassion and healing.

Focus on progress, not perfection: There's no right or wrong way to grieve. Focus on making incremental steps towards healing, not being flawless.

By recognizing the many types of guilt in mourning and adopting healthy coping methods, you may begin to unwind the knot of self-blame and discover a route towards self-compassion and acceptance. Remember, you are not alone on this path. There is help available, and you have the strength to go on with love and forgiveness.

This chapter serves as a guide, but remember, your sorrow is unique. Embrace the trip, manage the waves with courage, and know that you are not alone in this storm.

Additional Resources:
The National Alliance for Grieving Children &
Families: [https://www.childrengrieve.org/]

The Dougy Center: [https://www.dougy.org/]

The Center for Loss & Life Transition:
[https://www.centerforloss.com/]

Hoping this chapter provides you helpful insights
and assistance as you traverse the waves of loss.

Chapter 3:

Everyone Grieves Differently: Embracing the Mosaic of Loss

Grief, like a snowflake, is unique and complex. While the grief of loss may be universal, the manner we express and negotiate it is as unique as the human experience itself. This chapter honors the distinctiveness of sorrow, investigating the causes behind its diverse expressions and encourages us to accept its rich tapestry.

1. Understanding the Roots of Uniqueness:

Grief, the emotional response to loss, is a complicated and diverse process that varies widely from person to person. While there may be some general themes and phases linked with grieving, the individual manifestation of these emotions is distinct and impacted by a range of situations.

Individual Personalities:
Expression: Some persons are naturally open about their feelings, seeking support by chatting, sharing experiences, and engaging in group activities. Others find peace in isolation, writing,

or creative endeavors like painting or music. Recognizing this range of expression helps us avoid condemning or forcing someone to mourn in a way that seems unnatural to them.

Coping methods: Each individual develops their own coping methods, determined by personality and prior experiences. Some find comfort in rituals and structure, while others prefer diversion or novelty. Understanding these variances helps us to deliver support suited to their individual requirements.

Life Experiences: Past losses, traumas, and personal struggles might impact how someone grieves. Someone who has encountered repeated losses could have acquired strong coping skills, whereas someone fresh to sorrow may require more direction and assistance. Recognizing these distinct experiences builds empathy and understanding.

Nature of the Relationship: Emotional Weight: The depth and complexity of the link with the departed directly affects the severity and length of mourning. Losing a spouse, a child, or a close friend typically generates intense feelings and needs significant emotional processing. Recognizing the various weight of these relationships helps us to give appropriate degrees of assistance.

Unique Memories & Rituals: The nature of the connection determines the memories and rituals involved with sorrow. Mourning a parent could require preserving family traditions, whereas mourning a friend might involve reliving shared events or places. Respecting these distinct expressions of mourning is vital.

Cultural Background: Public vs. Private Expression: Some cultures have extensive public displays of grief, including rituals, ceremonies, and communal meetings. Others advocate more private manifestations of mourning inside the family. Understanding these cultural variations helps us avoid putting our own expectations on others.

Religious & Spiritual Beliefs: Cultural standards are typically connected with religious and spiritual beliefs, which can bring solace and meaning during bereavement. Some cultures emphasize rituals and prayers, while others emphasize acceptance and letting go. Respecting these varied perspectives develops understanding and support.

Personal Beliefs: Religious & Spiritual Practices: Religious or spiritual beliefs can give unique sources of consolation and strength during bereavement. Some individuals find peace in rituals and prayers, while others gain strength from a belief in an afterlife. Respecting these personal views is vital in aiding someone's grief process.

Meaning-Making: Grieving frequently entails looking for meaning and comprehending the loss. Personal beliefs might help individuals make sense of the experience and find peace. Supporting someone's investigation of their own belief system may be a helpful source of assistance.

Life Circumstances: Age & Health: Age and health can dramatically affect how someone grieves. A small kid grieving a parent may need different assistance than an elderly individual losing a spouse. Recognizing these variances helps us to personalize our service to their individual requirements and constraints.

Social Support & Resources: Access to social support and resources may dramatically affect how someone copes with bereavement. Having a strong support network of friends, family, or professionals may give vital emotional and practical aid. Recognizing and resolving any constraints in access to resources helps us to assist clients locate alternate sources of support.

Remember:
There is no "right" way to grieve. Each individual's experience is unique and deserves respect and understanding.

By recognizing the multiple sources of individuality in sorrow, we may give more tailored and effective care to persons who are grieving.

Be careful of your own prejudices and cultural preconceptions when assisting someone who is mourning.

Encourage open communication and listen carefully to their wants and preferences.

By embracing the mosaic of sorrow and honoring the different experiences of individuals, we may create a more helpful and understanding atmosphere for those who are traveling this tough road.

2. Celebrating Individualized Expressions of Loss:

There is no deadline for healing:
Embrace your own pace: Let go of cultural
pressure to "get over it" within a set timeframe.
Everyone's path is unique, and recognizing your
specific requirements is vital.

Validate your emotions: Allow yourself to feel the
whole gamut of emotions that arise, from grief
and rage to perplexity and even moments of
delight. There is no right or incorrect way to feel.

Be gentle to yourself: Treat yourself with love
and empathy throughout this challenging period.
Take care of your physical and mental health with
self-care habits including good food, exercise,
and relaxation techniques.

Honor your specific needs:
Seek assistance on your terms: Don't be hesitant
to ask for help, but pick the form of support that
seems most comfortable to you. Whether it's
talking to friends and family, attending a grieving
support group, or seeking professional
treatment, discover what works for you.

Explore uncommon expressions: Grieving can show in many ways. Don't shy away from expressing your feelings via creative avenues like writing, painting, music, or dance.

Maintain healthy routines: While acknowledging your desire for flexibility, keeping some structure and regularity in your daily life can bring stability and comfort during this hard time.

Embrace the gamut of emotions:
Normalize all feelings: Grief is not simply about sadness. Recognize that anger, guilt, perplexity, and even times of delight are legitimate components of the process. Allow yourself to feel these emotions without judgment.

Talk frankly about your feelings: Sharing your feelings with trusted loved ones or a therapist can give a safe space to process and comprehend your experience.

Seek expert help: If you're struggling to control your emotions or feel overwhelmed, don't hesitate to seek professional treatment from a therapist or counselor specialized in grieving.

Find healthy outlets:
Connect with nature: Spending time in nature can be immensely therapeutic and bring a sense of serenity and connection. Go on walks, stroll in the woods, or simply sit by a river and listen to the noises.

Engage in creative activities: Expressing oneself creatively may be a powerful method to manage emotions and find consolation.

Explore writing, painting, music, dancing, or any other creative medium that connects with you.

Do what you liked with them: If your loved one enjoyed a certain activity, consider finding ways to include it into your mourning process. Whether it's making a beloved meal, listening to their favorite music, or visiting locations you shared, these actions may keep their memory alive in a meaningful way.

Finding Your Voice:
Challenge cultural norms: Don't feel compelled to adhere to standards of how you "should" mourn. Your experience is unique, and expressing your feelings in ways that are true and relevant to you is crucial.

Let go of judgment: Don't condemn yourself or others for expressing grief differently. Celebrate the range of human emotions and allow yourself to feel yours without shame.

Find your tribe: Surround yourself with helpful individuals who appreciate and understand your specific experience. Seek out individuals who have experienced loss or join online forums for shared experiences and encouragement.

Honoring Memories in Unique Ways:
Create customized rituals: Traditional funerals may not resonate with everyone. Consider establishing bespoke rituals that celebrate your loved one's life and ideals. This might be planting a tree in their memory, organizing a potluck with their favorite cuisine, or penning letters full of memories and releasing them into the air.

Visit cherished places: Revisit areas that carried significance for your loved one, whether it's their favorite park, beach, or childhood home. These encounters might awaken cherished memories and create a sense of connection.

Keep their memories alive: Find strategies to keep your loved one's memory alive in a way that seems significant to you. This might be creating a charity in their honor, sharing tales about them with others, or just keeping onto a loved piece that belonged to them.

Finding Comfort in Unexpected Places:
Be open to new experiences: Don't limit yourself to traditional types of comfort. Explore alternative pathways and be open to finding peace in unexpected places. This might mean trying a new activity, attending a grieving program, or just spending time with a pet.

Connect with nature: Spending time in nature may be immensely healing. Go on walks, stroll in the woods, or simply sit by a river and listen to the noises.

Seek help from unexpected sources: You could receive comfort and understanding from unexpected sources, such as a trustworthy neighbor, a religious leader, or even an internet support group. Don't hesitate to reach out to folks you feel close to.

Remember, there is no one-size-fits-all strategy to mourning. By accepting your particular requirements, recognizing your

Examples of Diverse Expressions of Grief:
Grief, like a kaleidoscope, unfolds in a spectrum of bright and distinct ways. Each individual navigates loss via a prism created by their personality, experiences, and cultural background. Recognizing and valuing these varied manifestations of sorrow is vital for delivering sensitive and effective assistance.

Here, we go deeper into some popular examples:

The Quiet Grieve:
Internal Processing: These persons find peace in introspective thinking, writing, or spending time alone in nature. They may show their sadness via quiet weeping, seclusion, or alterations in their customary habits.

Respectful Support: Avoid pressing them to communicate or interact if they prefer alone. Offer assistance by ensuring they have access to nutritious food, a secure area to grieve, and someone to listen when they're ready.

Examples: Sitting silently at a loved one's favorite area, visiting their cemetery alone, or composing letters conveying unsaid emotions.

The Expressive Grieve: Open Communication: These persons find healing in communicating their feelings freely with loved ones, support groups, or therapists. They may publicly express their despair, anger, perplexity, or even times of elation by talking, sobbing, or laughter.

Active Listening: Create a secure environment for them to express themselves without judgment. Actively listen, provide affirmation, and avoid diminishing their emotions.

Examples: Talking freely with friends and family, attending a bereavement support group, or seeking individual treatment to process their emotions.

The Ritualistic Grieve: Finding Meaning: Creating and following certain rituals might provide comfort and structure to their grief experience. These rituals could entail visiting the cemetery regularly, lighting candles on anniversaries, or partaking in activities their loved one enjoyed.

Respecting Traditions: Recognize the relevance of these traditions in their healing path. Avoid criticizing their customs or seeking to modify them unless they demonstrate interest in doing so voluntarily.

Examples: Planting a memorial garden, attending religious services in their remembrance, or making their favorite food on important occasions.

The Action-Oriented Grieve: Channeling Emotions: Some persons find peace in channeling their sorrow into action. This could be volunteering for issues their loved one cared about, arranging events in their memory, or engaging in activities that encourage healing and growth.

Finding Purpose: Support their efforts to relate their sadness to meaningful action. Help them locate possibilities that connect with their beliefs and the memory of their loved one.

Examples: Participating in charity walks in their loved one's honor, founding a foundation dedicated to their cause, or mentoring others who have had similar losses.

Remember: No Single "Right" Way: Each individual's expression of grief is unique and valid. Avoid comparing them to others or placing your own expectations on their grief process.

Offer Personalized Support: Tailor your help to their individual needs and preferences. Some may require more distance, while others may seek greater closeness.

Be Patient and Understanding: Grief is a journey, not a destination. Be patient with their growth and aware of their developing requirements.

Seek Help When Needed: If their loss appears overpowering or they struggle to cope, urge them to seek professional treatment from a therapist or counselor specialized in grieving.

By recognizing and honoring the varied manifestations of sorrow, we can create a more supportive and caring atmosphere for people traveling this tough path. Remember, each individual's experience is unique, and acknowledging their needs and giving polite support is crucial to helping them recover in their own manner.

3. Supporting Those Who Grieve Differently:

When someone we care about endures loss, it's natural to want to give assistance. However, mourning is a complex and individual process, and what helps for one person might not be beneficial for another. Understanding the many ways individuals mourn and adapting your support accordingly is vital. Here's a thorough instruction on how to achieve that:

Active Listening with Empathy and Validation: Create a Safe Space: Let them know you're available to listen without judgment, expectations, or interruptions. This gives a secure refuge for them to express their feelings openly.

Practice Active Listening: Pay great attention to their words and nonverbal signs. Show real attention through eye contact, body language, and introspective remarks.

Validate their Feelings: Acknowledge the reality of their emotions, even if you don't entirely comprehend them. Phrases like "I see how much pain you're in" or "It's okay to feel angry/sad/scared" may be effective.

Avoid Minimizing or Comparing: Don't say anything like "Be strong" or "It could be worse." Avoid comparing their sadness to others' experiences, since it might devalue their particular anguish.

Respecting Boundaries and Offering Personalized
Support:
Assess their Needs: Observe their behavior and
speech to discover their desired degree of
interaction. Do they seem reclusive and require
space, or do they actively want discussion and
connection?

Offer Support Options: Instead of asking what
they need, provide other choices like conversing,
exchanging memories, going for a stroll, or
simply sitting in silence. This allows them to pick
what feels most comfortable.

Respect their Boundaries: If they deny your offer,
don't take it personally. Respect their desire for
space and promise them you're accessible when
they're ready.

Patience and Understanding: Grief is a Journey,
Not a Destination: Remind them that mending
takes time and there's no predetermined
schedule. Avoid pressing them to "get over it" or
"move on" before they're ready.

Validate their Progress: Acknowledge even
modest measures people take towards recovery,
like expressing their feelings or engaging in
activities they like again.

Be Patient with Setbacks: Grief may be a rollercoaster of emotions. Be patient with setbacks and tell them that it's natural to endure ups and downs.

Connecting them with Resources:
Suggest Support Groups: Sharing their story with people who understand may be immensely beneficial. Research local grieving support groups or online communities that cater to their special needs (e.g., death of a spouse, kid, pet).

Recommend Therapy: If they're hard to deal with, try offering professional treatment from a therapist specialized in bereavement. Offer to assist them identify a qualified specialist or accompany them to their initial visit.

Provide Online Resources: Share websites, articles, or applications that give knowledge and assistance on bereavement and coping techniques. Remember, internet information can be a valuable addition, but shouldn't replace expert aid.

Additional Tips:
Be cautious of your own prejudices: We all have varied experiences with grieving, and it's vital to be aware of your own biases and preconceptions.

Avoid transferring your own expectations into their grief process.

Offer practical help: Sometimes, the most useful thing you can do is offer practical aid with everyday duties like cooking, cleaning, or running errands. This can reduce some strain and allow them to focus on sorrow.

Remember simple gestures matter: Simple acts of kindness like sending a card, bringing over a meal, or lending a listening ear may make a major impact in their journey.

By following these recommendations and giving assistance in a way that respects their specific needs and preferences, you may provide a safe and supportive environment for them to manage their grief and begin to recover.

Note:
There's no competition in grief: Comparing your experience to others is counterproductive. Focus on your own journey and what feels appropriate for you.

Respect individual boundaries: Everyone grieves differently. Offer assistance, but don't push your own coping strategies on others.

Seek professional aid if needed: If your loss feels overwhelming or is interfering with your everyday life, don't hesitate to seek professional treatment from a therapist specialized in grieving.

By accepting the individuality of individual grieving journeys, we can create a more empathetic and supportive place for everyone navigating the complexity of loss. Remember, you are not alone, and your particular method of mourning is valid and worthy of respect.

This chapter serves as a beginning point, but remember, your grief narrative is yours to create. Embrace its distinctiveness, find comfort in varied manifestations, and know that you are not alone on this walk.

PART TWO:

Sharing the Journey: Embracing Grief Together

Loss. It's a word weighted with grief, leaving tracks of emptiness in its wake. But when that loss hits the lives of children, teenagers, and young adults, the echoes of anguish resound much deeper. "Sharing the Journey", the second part of this book "Whispers of Comfort" isn't simply a guide, it's a hand extended, providing sympathetic assistance on the journey of loss.

This section takes you through the terrain of loss, walking alongside people afflicted. Within its pages, you'll find peace in understanding the complexity of youthful grieving, learning skills to facilitate honest communication, and exploring strategies to treasure memories while seeking strength and support.
Chapter by chapter, "Sharing the Journey" unravels the threads of healing. In "Talking Helps," find great methods for fostering honest talks, allowing young folks to express their feelings openly.

"Remembering with Love" offers a loving embrace, assisting you and your loved ones in nurturing cherished memories via tales, activities, and important rituals.

But handling loss isn't a solo route. "Finding Support" illustrates the necessity of developing a robust network of care, showcasing the numerous sources of comfort accessible - from the loving embrace of family and friends to the counsel of specialists and the shared experience of support groups.

"Growing Through Loss" whispers a message of hope, displaying amazing examples of perseverance and personal growth birthed from the embers of loss.

This trip may be lined with sadness, but it's not one done alone. "Sharing the Journey in Whispers of Comfort" is a guide, a lighthouse in the storm, giving consolation, understanding, and practical skills to help you and your loved ones walk the path of recovery together.

Remember, mourning is a personal journey, and this book is only a guide. Open its pages with an open heart, ready to explore, learn, and most importantly, share the journey of sorrow with love and understanding.

This section speaks eloquently about the idea driving this work. Grief, especially for young hearts, may be crushing and lonely. This book doesn't promise to calm the storm, but rather attempts to give soft whispers of compassion and support, promoting a shared trek across the landscape of loss.

Talking Helps: This chapter goes beyond merely promoting communication. It digs into understanding the specific issues young individuals have in expressing their sadness. It gives specific age-appropriate tactics for launching talks, from open-ended questions to entertaining activities that can establish a safe environment for emotional expression. Additionally, it discusses the problems of communicating with diverse types, introverts and extroverts alike.

Remembering with Love: This chapter isn't only about preserving memories; it's about nurturing healing through recollection. It includes innovative suggestions for activities that memorialize the loved one, such as building memory boxes, sending letters, or planting a memorial garden. These rituals not only keep the memory alive but also give a practical outlet for sadness and a sense of control over the situation.

Finding Support: This chapter extends beyond identifying resources. It highlights the need of developing a tailored support network that responds to the individual's requirements. It analyzes the benefits of numerous support systems, from the unconditional love of family to the skilled assistance of therapists and the shared understanding of bereavement support groups. It also teaches young persons self-advocacy skills, encouraging them to seek the help they need and feel comfortable doing so.

Growing Through Loss: This chapter doesn't shy away from the grief of loss, but it offers a light of hope. It displays real-life experiences of individuals who have not only survived but prospered despite enduring great loss. These tales highlight the possibility for human growth and perseverance, acting as a source of inspiration and encouragement for people on their own recovery journeys.

The section expands beyond specific chapters, stressing the interconnectivity of various ideas. It understands that discussing honestly may lead to more meaningful recall, that having support increases resilience, and that remembering with love can pave the path for personal progress. It invites readers to approach the book not as a linear guide, but as a toolbox replete with customisable tools and ideas.

Ultimately, "Sharing the Journey in Whispers of Comfort" is a testimonial to the power of understanding, compassion, and shared experiences in negotiating the tough terrain of bereavement. It whispers not just to young persons enduring loss but also to the adults who love and support them, providing a chorus of understanding and optimism that echoes throughout the journey.

Chapter 4:

Talking Helps: A Dive into Open Communication

This chapter serves as a cornerstone of the book "Sharing the Journey in Whispers of Comfort," understanding that open communication is vital for negotiating the complexity of loss, especially for young persons. It goes further, giving practical advice and tactics to support honest interactions and facilitate emotional expression.

1. Breaking the Silence:

Understanding Challenges of Grieving Youth
This chapter clearly understands that opening talks about sorrow with young individuals isn't always easy. Understanding the individual issues people experience is vital for providing a secure and supportive atmosphere where free conversation may develop. Let's go deeper into these difficulties based on age groups:

Younger Children (4-8 years old):
Limited Vocabulary and Understanding: Young children may not completely comprehend the notion of dying or have the language to describe

their thoughts. They can confuse it with sleep or separation.

Fear of Upsetting Others: They can worry about expressing the incorrect thing or making grownups upset, leading to quiet or avoidance.

Regression in Behavior: Regression to previous behaviors like thumb-sucking or bedwetting might be a means of expressing their emotional anguish.

Focus on Concrete Concerns: They could dwell on practical problems like "Will I see them again?" or "Who will take care of me now?"

Strategies:
Use age-appropriate terminology and describe death in simple terms.

Read children's books on loss and grief together.

Encourage children to express themselves via play, sketching, or storytelling.

Use clear examples and graphics to illustrate the topic.

Validate their fears and give reassurance and support.

Pre-Teens (9-12 years old):
Confusion and Uncertainty: They could experience contradicting feelings including grief, rage, guilt, and uncertainty, making it difficult to describe them.

Social Comparisons and Pressure: They could compare their grieving to others, leading to feelings of isolation or inadequacy.

Fear of Judgment: They could worry about being evaluated by their peers for expressing their feelings.

Physical Manifestations: They could encounter physical symptoms including headaches, stomachaches, or sleep issues.

Strategies:
Create safe settings for open and honest interactions.

Offer multiple channels for expression, such writing, art therapy, or group discussions.

Normalize the experience of mourning and validate their sentiments.

Help them identify and control their emotions through coping skills like relaxation techniques or exercise.

Encourage them to connect with supportive peers who understand their grief.

Teens (13-18 years old):
Withdrawal and Isolation: They could withdraw from friends and family, preferring to deal with their sadness alone.

Anger and Frustration: They could express their sadness via anger aimed at themselves, others, or the circumstance.

Bargaining and Denial: They could indulge in magical thinking or denial as a strategy to cope with the suffering.

Identity Crisis: Grieving a loved one can test their sense of self and their place in the world.

Strategies:
Respect their desire for space but stay accessible for talk when they are ready.

Acknowledge their rage and frustration and give appropriate channels for expression.

Gently address denial and push them to face the truth in a helpful way.

Help them examine their thoughts and identities via artistic activities, writing, or individual therapy.

Connect them with peer support groups or online forums where they can find understanding and connection.

Societal Expectations:
Beyond age-specific obstacles, the chapter should also address the wider social norms that often limit frank discussion about loss.

These include:
Stoicism: The expectation to be tough and conceal emotions, especially for guys, can lead to solitude and unresolved pain.

Fear of Talking About Death: The taboo around death might make it difficult to have open and honest talks.

Misconceptions about Grief: Myths like "time heals all wounds" or "grief should look a certain way" can generate false expectations and pressure to conform.

By recognizing these issues and cultural circumstances, adults can be better equipped to establish a secure and supportive atmosphere where young persons feel comfortable expressing their sorrow, allowing them to begin the healing process in a healthy and meaningful way.

1. Creating Safe places: This chapter highlights the vital importance of safe places in facilitating open discussion about grieving for children and teenagers.
It takes a deeper into constructing such havens, highlighting the significance of fostering trust and understanding.
Let's study these components in further detail:

Active Listening: This goes beyond merely hearing speech. It requires:

Full Attention: Put aside distractions, focus on the individual, and make eye contact to indicate your presence and attention.

Reflection and Summarization: Briefly restate what you hear, indicating you understand and validating their emotions. "So you're feeling sad and confused about what happened?"

Nonverbal Cues: Pay attention to body language and facial emotions. Offer a consoling touch or a reassuring nod to recognize their sentiments.

Open-Ended inquiries: Instead of leading inquiries, promote elaboration with statements like "Tell me more about that," or "What else can you tell me about how you're feeling?"

2. Validating Feelings:
Acknowledge All Emotions: Don't condemn or belittle their sentiments, especially if they appear intense or "negative." "It's okay to be angry, and it's understandable that you're scared."

Normalize Their Experience: Share examples of how others cope with comparable losses, emphasizing that their sentiments are normal and shared by many.

Focus on Understanding: Instead of providing platitudes, attempt to understand the basis of their emotions. Ask inquiries like "What makes you feel this way?" or "What would help you feel better?"

3. Avoiding Forced Positivity:
Respect the Pain: Grief is a complicated journey with highs and lows. Don't attempt to push positivism or diminish their grief with platitudes like "Everything happens for a reason."

Provide Comfort and Empathy: Acknowledge the hardship of their position and provide words of comfort and support. "This is a hard time, but you're not alone."

Focus on optimism: While acknowledging the grief, provide a glimpse of optimism for the future. "Things might not be easy right now, but we'll get through this together."

4. Offering Choices and Respecting Boundaries:
Empowerment is Key: Give them control over how and when they want to talk. Offer possibilities like one-on-one chats, group discussions, writing in a diary, or engaging in creative activities.

Respect Their Pace: Don't urge them to talk if they're not ready. Allow for stillness and accept their desire for space.

Boundaries are Important: Teach children about healthy boundaries and encourage them to convey their demands assertively. "I'm not comfortable talking about this right now, but I appreciate your offer."

5. Additional Considerations:
Age-Appropriate Strategies: Tailor your approach to their growth stage. Younger children could benefit from play therapy or storytelling, while adolescents might prefer journaling or group discussions.

Cultural and Religious Sensitivity: Be cognizant of varied cultural and religious ideas regarding death and bereavement. Involve family members or community leaders in developing a safe area that accords with their traditions.

Nonverbal Communication: Pay attention to nonverbal signs, especially in younger children who can struggle to express themselves vocally. Observe changes in behavior, sleep patterns, or food habits.

Professional Help: If they seem overwhelmed or struggle to cope, advise obtaining professional treatment from therapists specialized in childhood and teenage grieving.

Remember, building a safe place is an ongoing endeavor. Be patient, adaptable, and change your approach as needed. By building trust, understanding, and open conversation, you may help them break the silence of loss and go on a road of recovery in a supportive atmosphere. Beginning talks: Here we highlight the necessity of beginning talks about grieving, but admit the complexity of finding the correct technique for different age groups.

Let's discuss particular features and techniques to ignite open conversation with young individuals:

Younger Children (4-8 years old):
Open-Ended Questions: Avoid leading questions that indicate certain replies. Instead, use suggestions like "What do you remember most about [loved one]?" or "What worries you the most about what happened?"

Storytelling and Play Therapy: Use children's books on loss, write tales together, or employ puppets to act out events. This helps individuals to express their feelings indirectly and explore challenging subjects in a safe and sympathetic way.

Activities & Rituals: Engage them in activities like painting memories, establishing a memorial garden, or building a memory box. These rituals give physical outlets for mourning and a real method to connect with the loved one.

Respecting Their Play: Remember, play is their primary language. Observe their play patterns for signs about their emotional condition and use play therapy strategies to gently explore their feelings.

Pre-Teens (9-12 years old):
Share Your Own Story: If comfortable, share a personal experience of loss to open the way for them to share theirs. Normalize the experience of grief and demonstrate that it's normal to talk about it.

Discuss Movies/Books: Watch age-appropriate movies or read books dealing with sorrow together. Use these fictional narratives as springboards to examine their own thoughts and experiences.

Creative ideas: Offer journaling ideas like "Write a letter to [loved one]," or encourage them to depict how they feel inside. Creative expression can help them handle feelings that might be hard to convey verbally.

Group Discussions: Consider attending a grief support group particularly geared for pre-teens. Being among people who understand their situation may be immensely affirming and promote conversation.

Teens (13-18 years old):
Open Forum Discussions: Create a secure environment for honest and open interactions, free from judgment. Allow them to discuss their anger, bewilderment, or any other feelings they might be experiencing.

Connect Through Shared things: Engage in things they like, such playing games, listening to music, or going on walks. These common experiences can establish a forum for informal talks about sorrow.

Explore Online Resources: Encourage them to explore online forums or social media groups for teenagers suffering with loss. Connecting with peers online may give anonymity and a feeling of community.

Respect Their Independence: While giving assistance, respect their desire for independence and space. Be accessible for talks when they begin them, but avoid pressuring them to communicate before they're ready.

Additional Tips:
Tailor to Individual Needs: Consider their personality, hobbies, and cultural background when considering communication tactics.

Validate Their Responses: Avoid rejecting their sentiments as "dramatic" or "overreacting." Listen actively and recognize their unique viewpoint on the loss.

Be Patient: Building trust and beginning open conversation takes time. Be patient and enable them to open up at their own speed.

Seek Professional Help: If they seem overwhelmed or unable to cope, don't hesitate to offer professional treatment from a therapist specialized in teenage grieving.

Remember, beginning discussions is about providing a safe environment for free communication, not demanding predetermined conclusions. By adopting these age-appropriate tactics and exhibiting real compassion, you may enable children to express their sadness and begin their healing journey.

2. Tailoring Communication: A Spectrum of Approaches for Diverse Grievers

"Talking Helps" goes beyond merely advocating open communication; it argues for adapting communication to the particular requirements of each young person. Let's go deeper into addressing individual variances, cultural factors, and handling challenging emotions:

Addressing Individual Differences:
Introverts vs. Extroverts:
Introverts: Offer one-on-one chats, writing prompts, or individual creative activities like art therapy or music creation. Encourage them to communicate their feelings at their own speed, respecting their need for introspection and isolation.

Extroverts: Facilitate group conversations, involve them in physical activities like sports or hikes, or role-playing scenarios to explore different emotions. Encourage open expression and create opportunities for them to share their ideas with others.

Learning Styles: Consider their chosen learning styles. Some might respond better to visual assistance like memory boxes or picture albums, while others could benefit from aural resources like listening to music or podcasts about mourning.

Personality qualities: Recognize how their personality qualities impact their communication style. Some could be more analytical and prefer factual talks, while others might be more emotional and find comfort in expressing sentiments openly.

Cultural Considerations in Grief Communication
The chapter appropriately stresses recognizing and utilizing cultural viewpoints while aiding young persons through bereavement. Let's investigate this key topic in even more detail:

Understanding the Spectrum of Cultural Practices:
Research and Learn: Familiarize yourself with the varied beliefs and practices around death and sorrow within their individual cultural background. This includes grieving rituals, funeral traditions, special language used to convey loss, and any taboos or sensitivities to consider.

Seek Guidance: Don't shy away from asking inquiries regarding their cultural customs. Consult community leaders, religious figures, or cultural experts to obtain deeper insight and avoid inadvertent blunders.

Acknowledge Differences: Recognize that cultural behaviors differ widely, even between seemingly similar populations. Avoid drawing generalizations and enjoy the individuality of their customs.

Integrating Traditions into Communication: Incorporate Rituals: If appropriate, participate in or encourage their involvement in culturally meaningful rituals like wakes, prayers, or special memorial activities. This communicates respect and creates a feeling of normalcy within their cultural context.

Relate Tales: Encourage children to relate tales about departed ancestors, cultural figures, or their own recollections using culturally appropriate language and terminology. This creates connection to their ancestry and gives comfort via shared narratives.

Acknowledge Cultural Values: Consider how their cultural values impact their mourning experience.

For example, collectivistic cultures can stress collective support, whereas individualistic cultures might promote personal expression. Tailor your speech to match with these principles.

Navigating Sensitive Topics:
Open and Respectful Dialog: When discussing culturally sensitive themes like afterlife beliefs or specialized grieving traditions, do so freely and politely. Avoid judging or imposing your own opinions, and stress actively listening to their perspectives.

Address Taboos: If aware of any cultural taboos associated with death or mourning, be alert not to break them through your words or behavior. Seek counsel from reliable members within their community if unsure.

Give Alternatives: If some traditional activities are not viable owing to individual choices or circumstances, give alternative methods to honor their cultural beliefs and express their grief.

Additional Considerations:
Family Dynamics: Involve family members or trustworthy adults from their cultural background in the communication process, especially if handling challenging issues or enabling customs.

Respecting Individual Choices: While preserving traditional customs, recognize that individual comfort and preferences ultimately count. Listen to their voice and give alternatives within the cultural context that feel real to them.

Professional Help: If cultural differences present extra obstacles, seek professional help from therapists or counselors experienced with varied cultural origins and specialized in childhood and teenage grief.

By adopting cultural sensitivity and actively incorporating their traditions into communication, you may provide a safe and supportive environment for young persons to express their sorrow authentically, connecting them to their cultural origins while helping their recovery path.

Remember, cultural concerns are not an add-on; they are crucial to understanding and helping people through this tough time.

Navigating Difficult Emotions:Helping Young Grievers Express Difficult Emotions

Grief isn't always a smooth flow of grief. Anger, anger, and guilt may erupt like storm waves, leaving young folks overwhelmed and bewildered. "Talking Helps" understands this, pushing adults to not only normalize these feelings but also empower themselves with strategies to manage them. Let's go more into this vital aspect:

Normalization: Validating the Emotional Storm

Start with Empathy: Acknowledge their emotions without judgment. Phrases like "It's completely understandable to feel angry after such a loss" or "Guilt is a common reaction to grief, but remember you're not to blame" affirm their experience and offer a safe space for expression.

Challenge society Stigmas: Discuss how society norms like "be strong" can make expressing painful emotions feel improper. Explain that these sentiments are natural and healthy components of the mourning process.

Normalize Intensity: Don't downplay the severity of their feelings. Phrases like "It's okay to feel sad, even if it feels overwhelming" or "It's normal to be angry sometimes, even at the person you lost" give room for individuals to embrace and process their feelings honestly.

Providing Healthy Outlets: Expressing the Storm Within Creative Expression: Offer creative outlets like painting, music, writing, or dancing. These media allow them to communicate feelings nonverbally, explore uncomfortable concepts, and achieve catharsis without being constrained by words.

Physical Activity: Encourage physical activity like sports, exercise, or outdoor trips. These outlets can help relieve pent-up emotions, channel irritation in a healthy way, and enhance their general well-being.

Journaling: Provide them with a secure environment to express their ideas and feelings through journaling. Prompt them with questions like "What are you feeling right now?" or "What do you miss most about [loved one]?"

Role-Playing: Explore scenarios where kids may express their tough emotions in a safe and regulated way. This can help children understand their feelings better and build good coping methods.

Addressing Underlying Concerns: Untangling the Knots of Emotion
Active Listening: Listen actively and intently when people express anger, frustration, or guilt. Ask open-ended inquiries like "What makes you feel angry?" or "Can you tell me more about why you feel guilty?" to grasp the basis of their feelings.

Cognitive Restructuring: Help them fight negative thought processes that generate shame or self-blame. Gently assist them to see the event honestly and appreciate that they might not have had control over what happened.

Focus on Positive Actions: Encourage them to conduct good deeds in remembrance of the loved one or to support others going through similar situations. This might empower them and redirect their painful feelings into something valuable.

Offering Reassurance and Support: A Steady Anchor amid the Storm
Patience and Understanding: Remember, managing sorrow requires time and patience. Don't expect them to "get over it" immediately.

Be mindful of their emotional ups and downs, and give steady support throughout the trip. Reassurance and Empathy: Offer reassuring words like "You're not alone in this" or "I'm here for you, no matter what." Let them know they can come to you with whatever feelings they might be experiencing.

Professional Help: If their feelings become overpowering or interfere with their everyday life, urge them to seek professional treatment from a therapist specialized in children and teenage grief.

Additional Considerations:
Age-Appropriate Strategies: Tailor your approach based on their age and developmental stage. Younger children could benefit from simpler hobbies like sketching or playing, while adolescents might prefer writing or talking through their feelings.

Cultural Sensitivity: Consider their cultural background and ideas regarding bereavement and emotional expression. Respect their cultural conventions and modify your approach accordingly.

Self-Care for Adults: Remember to take care of yourself emotionally. Supporting someone through sorrow may be stressful, so ensure you have your own outlets for processing emotions and preserving your well-being.

By providing a secure location, acknowledging their emotions, and offering healthy channels for expression, you may assist young individuals navigate the storm of unpleasant emotions during mourning.

Remember, patience, understanding, and unwavering support are vital anchors in this path towards healing.

Additional Tips:
Observe and Adapt: Pay attention to their nonverbal clues and change your communication approach accordingly. If they look overloaded by verbal communication, turn to creative activities or simply provide a listening ear.

Collaboration is Key: Work with their teachers, counselors, or other trusted adults to build a consistent and supportive communication method across diverse situations.

Seek Professional Help: If they struggle to manage tough feelings on their own, consider obtaining professional treatment from therapists specialized in children and teenage mourning. Remember, personalizing communication is a continual effort. Observe their replies, change your approach based on their requirements, and most importantly, establish a secure atmosphere where they feel comfortable expressing themselves genuinely and begin their recovery journey.

3. Beyond Words: Exploring UnSpoken Grief

In this chapter, we realizes that grieving isn't always contained to words. Often, the deepest feelings lay beyond language, communicated through subtle clues and artistic means. Let's go deeper into the power of nonverbal communication, creative outlets, and seeking professional support:

Unlocking the Nonverbal Language:
Beyond Words: Observe their body language, facial expressions, and changes in behavior. A stooped posture, downcast gaze, or increased fidgeting might suggest sorrow or worry. Look for changes in sleep patterns, food habits, or interest in activities they used to like.

Playing it Out: Play therapy can be particularly useful for younger children who struggle to express themselves verbally. Observe their play patterns, themes, and choices to understand their emotional condition. Do they create sorrowful structures or sketch lonely figures? Use play to gently explore their feelings and give comfort.

Art as Expression: Encourage sketching, painting, or constructing activities. These nonverbal media allow children to convey emotions they might not have words for. Analyze their creations to acquire insights into their sentiments and give advice without judgment.

Creative Catharsis: A Journey of Expression Finding Their Voice: Writing poetry, novels, or even song lyrics may give an avenue for processing complicated emotions. Encourage them to write letters to the departed, vent their anger via fictitious characters, or simply write down their thoughts and feelings without expectations.

Melody of Grief: Music therapy may be immensely effective. Encourage them to produce music, listen to songs that resonate with their emotions, or even utilize music improvisation to explore their feelings in a non-verbal way.

Theatrical Release: Role-playing, drama therapy, or even participating in plays may give a safe environment to explore emotions, articulate tough experiences, and acquire useful insight.

Seeking Professional Support: When Words Aren't Enough
Recognizing the Need: Some folks may require more help beyond what you can supply. Signs like persistent melancholy, social disengagement, academic challenges, or self-harm suggest the need for professional care.

Open Communication: Talk freely about obtaining professional help. Normalize therapy and explain how it may offer them tools to cope with bereavement and regulate their emotions appropriately.

Finding the Right Fit: Work with them to identify a therapist specialized in childhood and teenage grief who knows their cultural background and specific requirements. Consider online therapy choices if accessibility is an issue.

Additional Considerations:
Age-Appropriate Approaches: Tailor your methods based on their age and developmental stage. Younger children could benefit from more controlled activities like play therapy or art projects, while adolescents might prefer open-ended creative projects or individual therapy sessions.

Cultural Sensitivity: Be conscious of cultural perceptions on sorrow and expressiveness. Encourage them to employ creative outlets that resonate with their cultural traditions and beliefs.

Self-Care for Adults: Supporting someone through sorrow needs emotional resilience. Practice self-care by maintaining healthy behaviors, getting help from your own network, and remembering to prioritize your well-being.

By recognizing the power of nonverbal communication, supporting creative expression, and giving professional help when required, you may become a beacon of compassion and support for young persons navigating the unknown seas of loss. Remember, sometimes, the most deep healing comes outside the limitations of language.

Remember:
Patience is Key: Grieving is a process, not an event. Be patient and empathetic, allowing folks to talk when they are ready and respecting their pace.

Active Listening Matters: Pay attention not just to words but also to feelings. Listen without judgment, validate feelings, and provide support without pressing answers.

Empowerment is Essential: Encourage children and teenagers to express themselves in ways that seem comfortable for them. Provide alternatives, affirm their feelings, and strengthen their confidence in voicing their needs.

By combining these tactics from this chapter, adults may become trusted partners on the path of grieving, enabling open conversation and emotional expression that are necessary for healing and growth.

Chapter 5:

Remembering with Love: Honoring Their Memory Through Stories, Activities, and Shared Rituals

In the wake of loss, sorrow can feel overwhelming, especially for children, teenagers, and young adults. While there's no one-size-fits-all way to traverse this tough road, this chapter delivers a strong message: remembering with love may be a source of healing and connection. It dives into methods to celebrate the memory of the loved one via tales, activities, and shared traditions, establishing a sense of connection and maintaining their legacy.

1. The Power of Storytelling: Sharing Memories in Detail

Here, the power of storytelling takes center stage as a key tool for children and teenagers to negotiate loss and connect with the memories of their loved one. Here's how you may stimulate and deepen this crucial process:

Beyond Recalling:
Prompt with open-ended questions:
Instead of conventional "what was their favorite color?" inquiry, dive deeper with prompts like "Tell me about a time they made you laugh so hard you cried," or "What was something unique about the way they did things?"

Create a memory map: Gather artifacts reflecting different elements of the loved one's life (hobbies, work, passions) and use them as triggers for narrative. Each thing might inspire a fresh recollection or lead to further research of their characteristics.

Use sensory details: Encourage students to construct a vivid image with their words. How did their loved one's laugh? What was the material of their favorite chair? What fragrances remind them of them?

Interactive Storytelling:
Play memory games: Create a memory bingo card with photos or terms relating to the loved one. Share tales to fill the squares, promoting laughter and connection.

Write a collaborative story: Start a tale about the loved one together, taking turns adding phrases or paragraphs. This allows everyone to offer their own perspective and recollections.

Record memories: Encourage youngsters and teenagers to film themselves narrating tales about the loved one. This produces a lasting keepsake and allows people to relive these moments in the future.

Tangible Memories:
Memory boxes: As advised, construct personalized memory boxes. Include photographs, handwritten notes, little artifacts, and even recordings of stories. Encourage decorating the box to represent the loved one's individuality.

Scrapbooks or picture albums: Create visual scrapbooks or albums packed with images, souvenirs, and written narrative. This gives a practical means to recall memories and share them with others.

Digital memory boards: Utilize internet platforms to build digital memory boards with photographs, videos, and written tributes. This may be a collaborative activity and easily shared with extended family and friends.

Remember:
Adapt to age and interests: Tailor storytelling activities to the individual age and developmental level of each kid or teen. Younger children could like simpler games and crafts, while older adolescents might prefer deeper talks and creative writing projects.

Listen actively: Provide a secure and supportive venue for people to express their tales without judgment. Show genuine curiosity and offer follow-up questions to generate comprehensive storytelling.

Be careful of emotions: Sharing memories can trigger a range of emotions, from pleasure and laughter to grief and wrath. Validate all emotions and enable them to express themselves freely.

By developing a culture of storytelling within your family, you may encourage children and teenagers to not only grieve but also celebrate the life and legacy of their loved one. These shared experiences become threads that weave together remembrance, love, and healing,

ensuring that the light of their loved one
continues to shine brightly.

Reading Stories Together: Finding Comfort and
Insight in Shared Narratives
This chapter underscores the essential impact
shared reading can have in aiding children and
teenagers experiencing sorrow. Here are some
ways to pick and debate books in a meaningful
way:

Choosing the Right Books:
Consider age and maturity: Select books suited
for the child's cognitive stage and capacity to
grasp complicated emotions. Younger children
could benefit from picture books with basic
storylines, while older adolescents can manage
more sophisticated and realistic representations
of sorrow.

Themes and feelings: Look for works that relate
with the unique sort of loss experienced and
explore emotions including grief, rage, perplexity,
and acceptance.

Representation: Choose novels that represent
the child's or teen's history and identity,
providing a sense of connection and
understanding.

Facilitating Meaningful Discussions:
Create a safe space: Before reading, highlight that there are no right or wrong responses during discussion and promote open communication.

Read together: Take turns reading loudly or have everyone read separately depending on age and desire.

Engage with the characters: Ask questions about how the characters are feeling, how they cope with their loss, and what makes them happy or sad.

Relate to personal experiences: Gently tie the story's themes to the child's or teen's personal experiences, allowing them to communicate their ideas and feelings without pressure.

Focus on hope and healing: While acknowledging the sadness of loss, stress positive themes like perseverance, hope, and finding strength in loved ones and memories.

Book Recommendations:
For Younger Children:
The Invisible String by Patrice Karavita:
A heartwarming story about an unseen line
linking loved ones, even after death.

The Memory Box by Joanna Rowland: Explores
the role of memories and treasures in coping
with bereavement.

I Miss You! A First Look at Grief by Marianne
Cummins: Offers straightforward explanations
and reassurance for young children who have
lost someone.

For Middle Grade Readers:
Number the Stars by Lois Lowry:
A fictional narrative about heroism and loss
during World War II that gives historical
background and examines themes of family and
perseverance.

Bridge to Terabithia by Katherine Paterson:
A moving tale of friendship, grief, and
coming-of-age that teaches about empathy and
dealing with unpleasant emotions.

Goodbye Days by Jason Reynolds:
A graphic novel follows a young kid facing the
untimely death of his father through anger,
uncertainty, and finally, acceptance.

For Teens:
All the Bright Places by Jennifer Niven: Explores
topics of despair, suicide, and sorrow through the
eyes of two teens grappling with their own
difficulties.

Cinder by Marissa Meyer:
A science fiction reworking of Cinderella set in a
dystopian future, giving a compelling getaway
while examining issues of loss, identity, and
hope.

The Perks of Being a Wallflower by Stephen
Chbosky:
A touching coming-of-age narrative about
negotiating friendship, love, and loss in high
school, confronting topics of depression and
mental health.

Remember, these are only a few
recommendations, and the greatest novels are
ones that resonate with the kid or teen's specific
interests and experiences. By reading together
and engaging in open discussions, you may

develop a powerful tool for encouraging understanding, healing, and connection along their journey through loss.

Writing Stories: Exploring Emotions and Healing Through Imagination
In this chapter, writing stories emerges as another kind of storytelling with enormous promise for healing. Here's how you may inspire children and teenagers to express themselves via creative writing:

Exploring Different Formats:
Poems: Encourage composing brief, rhyming poems about the loved one, or explore free poetry to express feelings freely. Poems may capture transitory sensations and give a unique method to memorialize exceptional occasions.

Letters: Suggest sending letters to the loved one, explaining what they miss, things they wish they could say, or just expressing their present thoughts. These letters can serve as a therapeutic release and a means to grieve sorrow quietly.

Fictitious tales: Allow them to construct fictitious stories where the loved one is still there, exploring feelings, anxieties, and hopes in a safe and imagined setting. This may be a helpful tool for investigating "what if" situations and understanding their own feelings.

Prompting Creativity:
Offer beginning points: Provide ideas like "Write a story about a dream you had about your loved one," or "Imagine you could have one more conversation with them, what would you say?" These prompts can ignite inspiration and lead their writing journey.

Share writing activities: Engage in group writing projects like crafting a collaborative tale about the loved one's life, everyone taking turns contributing paragraphs. This stimulates creativity and creates bonds via shared memories.

Utilize writing tools: Introduce internet platforms or applications created for creative writing, allowing children to explore new styles and share their stories safely.

Creating a Safe Environment:
Emphasize no pressure: Reassure children that there are no right or incorrect stories, and they may write whatever seems natural and honest.

Respect privacy: Allow them to determine who they want to share their writing with, if anybody.

Offer feedback: Provide constructive feedback emphasizing on strengths and encouraging further inquiry, while respecting their emotional sensitivity.

Examples of Writing Prompts:
What was your loved one's favorite place? Write a narrative about a fantastic adventure you have there together.

If your loved one had a superpower, what would it be? Write a narrative where they use that power to aid others.

Close your eyes and imagine the happiest memory you have with your loved one. Now, create a tale about it.

Remember, writing may be a highly personal and therapeutic activity. By providing a secure environment and fostering discovery, you allow children and teenagers to express their unique feelings and find consolation in creation, eventually supporting their healing journey through sorrow.

2. Engaging Activities: Creating Memory Collages to Celebrate and Remember

This chapter also explores the significance of engaging activities in helping children and teenagers handle sorrow. Creating memory collages is a very important pastime as it provides for:

Creative Expression:

Gather varied materials: Collect pictures, drawings, magazine clippings, fabric scraps, buttons, ribbons, and any other artifacts that depict the loved one's personality, interests, and life path. Encourage innovation and personalization.

Experiment with layouts: Don't be scared to get dirty! Try alternative layouts, overlaying photographs, utilizing distinctive shapes for backdrops, and integrating handwritten words or quotations.

Express emotions via colors and textures: Choose colors that reflect the loved one's personality or feelings linked with them. Use multiple textures to give depth and interest to the collage.

Shared Memories and Laughter:
Involve family and friends: Make it a communal project! Invite family and friends to submit images, items, and tales. This generates shared memories, humor, and develops ties during the grief process.

Tell tales behind each item: Encourage everyone to share tales and memories linked with each thing they give. This establishes a stronger connection to the collage and keeps the loved one's memories alive.

Turn it into a game: Play memory games relating to the photographs or items included in the collage. This adds a fun factor and can help everyone discover new facts about the loved one.

Additional Tips:
Consider the age and interests: Tailor the exercise to the age and ability of the participants. Younger children could like simpler collages with huge images, while older adolescents can manage more complicated patterns and symbolic components.

Frame and display the collage: This offers a permanent memento of the loved one and can be a source of consolation and joy in the future.

Make digital collages: Utilize internet platforms or applications to make digital collages that can be readily shared with extended family and friends.

Remember:
Creating memory collages is not just about the finished product but also the process itself. It provides a secure and entertaining area for children and teenagers to express their feelings, exchange memories, and celebrate the life of their loved one. By stimulating creativity, cooperation, and humor, this exercise may be a powerful tool for healing and recollection.

Volunteering in Their Honor - Keeping Their Legacy Alive
This chapter highlights the relevance of engaging activities in helping children and teenagers cope with bereavement. Volunteering in honor of their loved one gives a unique approach to:

Find Purpose and Meaning:
Identify their passions: Reflect on the causes, activities, or organizations the loved one held dear. Was it animal welfare, environmental protection, assisting the disadvantaged, or something else?

Connect with their values: Choose a volunteering position that matches with the principles and beliefs the loved one treasured. This gives a feeling of purpose and helps people to feel linked to their legacy.

Make a good influence: By volunteering, children and teenagers contribute to a cause their loved one cares about, building a feeling of agency and positive impact in the community.

Connect with the Community and Heal Together: Involve family and friends: Make volunteering a communal activity, asking family and friends to join. This deepens connections, creates opportunity for shared experiences, and fosters a sense of support during the mourning process.

Meet new people: Volunteering connects children and teenagers to meet individuals who have similar interests and beliefs. This might generate a sense of belonging and build a support network outside their small group.

Learn and grow: Volunteering exposes individuals to new experiences, challenges, and viewpoints. This may foster personal growth, create self-confidence, and give vital life lessons.

Additional Tips:
Start small and adapt: Begin with short-term volunteering opportunities or one-time events to measure interest and comfort level. Adapt the exercise to their age and ability.

Focus on pleasant experiences: Choose possibilities that are likely to be entertaining and gratifying. Positive experiences can aid recovery and generate enduring memories.

Share their tale: If comfortable, encourage them to share their loved one's story with others while volunteering. This might attach people to the cause on a deeper level and encourage others.

Remember:
Volunteering in honor of a loved one may be a transforming experience for children and teenagers. It helps individuals to express their grief, connect with their loved one's ideals, and have a good influence on the world. By choosing meaningful initiatives and establishing a supportive environment, you may help them find comfort, purpose, and healing via volunteering.

Planting a Memory Garden - Cultivating Comfort and Remembrance

This chapter brilliantly shows the therapeutic value of building a living legacy through a memory garden. Here are some ideas to make this exercise relevant and interesting for children and teens:

Choosing Meaningful Plants:
Reflect on their personality: Select flowers, trees, or shrubs that remind you of the loved one's favorite colors, fragrances, or qualities. Were they energetic and outgoing? Choose bright, cheery blossoms. Were they quiet and peaceful? Opt for relaxing lavender or chamomile.

Consider symbolic meanings: Research the symbolic significance of different plants. Roses signify love, sunflowers reflect joy, and forget-me-nots stand for recollection. Choosing plants with specific value increases the bond to the loved one.

Involve them in the selection: Allow youngsters and teenagers to participate in picking the plants. This empowers them and ensures the garden symbolizes their personal relationship to the departed.

Creating a Special Space:
Design the layout together: Decide where the garden will be placed and sketch up a simple plan. Incorporate walkways, seats, or other items that promote spending time in the location.

Personalize it with mementos: Include modest, weatherproof artifacts that reflect the loved one, such as a favorite bird feeder, a painted rock with a personal inscription, or a wind chime with a comforting tune.

Make it interactive: Add elements like a bird bath, butterfly feeders, or a small water feature. Watching nature grow may offer consolation and establish a sense of connectedness to the living world.

Nurturing Growth and Remembrance:
Plant together: Make planting a communal effort. This generates shared experiences, teaches essential gardening skills, and instills a sense of responsibility for caring for the garden.

Hold frequent "garden visits": Encourage regular visits to the memory garden as a family. Use this opportunity to exchange tales, ponder on memories, and admire the growing plants.

Maintain the garden together: Caring for the plants together imparts vital lessons about responsibility, growth, and the cycles of life. It also offers a sense of achievement and reminds them of the ongoing existence of their loved one's memories.

Additional Tips:
Adapt for different ages: Tailor the complexity of the garden and activities to the skills and interests of children and teenagers. Younger children could enjoy basic planting jobs, while older adolescents might participate in more complicated design and upkeep initiatives.

Incorporate cultural traditions: Consider integrating flora or objects that bear cultural significance relating to your family's customs or beliefs.

Seek aid when needed: Don't hesitate to seek help from expert gardeners or local resources to guarantee the success of your memory garden.

Remember, establishing a memory garden is not only about the plants, but about providing a meaningful location for recollection, meditation, and healing. By incorporating children and teenagers in the process, you may develop a sense of connection to their loved one's memories, celebrate their life, and find consolation in the beauty of nature's growth.

3. Shared Rituals: Celebrating Birthdays and Anniversaries with Love

This chapter highlights the value of shared traditions in honoring the memory of a loved one. Birthdays and anniversaries may be particularly stressful times, but developing meaningful rituals can convert them into occasions of memory, love, and connection.

Finding Comfort in Traditions:
Gather loved ones: On birthdays and anniversaries, assemble relatives and friends who shared a relationship with the departed. This develops a sense of camaraderie and support during a tough moment.

Share cherished recollections: Encourage everyone to share their best memories of the loved one. Laughter and warm retellings can help relieve the sadness and commemorate their life.

Engage in familiar activities: If your loved one favored certain activities, add them into the gathering. Did they love baking? Have a cake-decorating session. Were they passionate about music? Organize a karaoke night with their favorite tunes.

Create new traditions: Consider developing new traditions that commemorate their memory. Plant a tree on their birthday, release floating lanterns with written messages on anniversaries, or give to their favorite charity in their honor.

Personalizing the Experience:
Adapt to individual needs: Allow room for varied methods of mourning and expressing feelings. Some may love a boisterous celebration, while others prefer peaceful introspection.

Create customized tributes: Write poetry, perform songs, or make presentations that demonstrate the particular link you enjoyed with the loved one.

Involve children and teens: Encourage children and teenagers to engage in age-appropriate ways. They can produce simple projects, send messages to the loved one, or share their best memories.
Additional Tips:

Be cognizant of religious and cultural traditions:
Consider integrating themes that resonate with
your family's values and cultural heritage.

Remember, there's no right or wrong way: Don't
feel forced to imitate earlier celebrations exactly.
Adapt the rituals to what feels comfortable and
meaningful for everyone participating.

Seek professional support: If sorrow gets
overwhelming, don't hesitate to seek professional
support from grief counselors or therapists.

Remember:
Celebrating birthdays and anniversaries can be a
melancholy experience, but it can also be a time
to connect with loved ones, share cherished
memories, and keep the spirit of the departed
alive. By building meaningful traditions and
maintaining a supportive environment, you may
convert these events into sources of comfort,
healing, and enduring love.

Finding Solace and Connection at the Gravesite
or Memorial
This stresses the vital significance visiting the
cemetery or memorial may have in the mourning

process. While feelings around this might be difficult, it can be a powerful space for shared rituals, quiet introspection, and finding peace in remembering your loved one.

Creating Meaningful Visits:
Plan as a family: Discuss what everyone intends to achieve from the visit and design activities that feel meaningful for everybody. This might be exchanging tales, singing songs, laying flowers or keepsakes, or simply spending time in peaceful thought.

Make it personal: Encourage participants to bring artifacts or images that have particular memories. Create a practice of exchanging treasured memories or anecdotes about the loved one.

Respect individual needs: Acknowledge that various family members may require different things from the visit. Some may desire to spend lengthy time in silent thought, while others may prefer quick, regular trips.

Finding Comfort in Traditions:
Establish frequent visits: Decide on a frequency that is appropriate for everyone, whether it's weekly, monthly, or on special events like

birthdays or anniversaries. Consistency may develop a sense of habit and comfort.

Create shared rituals: Develop significant customs customized to your household. This might include lighting candles, saying prayers, laying flowers, or releasing balloons with written messages.

Adapt to cultural and religious practices: Integrate aspects that resonate with your cultural or religious heritage, providing a sense of comfort and tranquility.

Additional Tips:
Be considerate of children's needs: Explain the goal of the visit in an age-appropriate manner and answer their questions honestly. Consider packing comfort things like cuddly animals or art tools.

Maintain the gravesite or memorial: Taking care of the place with gardening, cleaning, or adding decorations may be a gesture of respect and connection for certain families.
Seek professional support: If visiting the cemetery or memorial evokes extreme emotional discomfort, consider obtaining advice from a grieving counselor or therapist.

Remember:
Visiting the cemetery or memorial is not meant
to replace other kinds of grief but may be a
significant step in the healing process. By setting
meaningful rituals and maintaining a supportive
atmosphere, you may convert these visits into
powerful moments of shared recall, quiet
introspection, and finding peace in your loved
one's memories.

Weaving New Threads of Memory and Love
This discusses the significance of developing new
traditions to honor the memory of a loved one.
This isn't about replacing the past, but about
weaving new threads of recollection into the
fabric of your family's existence, honoring their
essence, and keeping their spirit strong.

Finding Inspiration in Their Passions:
Reflect on their interests: What pastimes,
hobbies, or traditions did they cherish? Did they
appreciate viewing old movies, crafting complex
pastries, or going on nature hikes?

Adapt and personalize: Adapt their favored
hobbies to the present family dynamic and
individual preferences. Perhaps you watch a
different classic movie each week, hold potlucks

with their trademark food, or include nature
hikes into regular family activities.

Go beyond the obvious: Think inventive! Did they
love a certain historical period? Organize a
themed dinner party. Were they enthusiastic
about a cause? Volunteer together in their name.

Establishing Meaningful Rituals:
Involve everyone: Create a venue where
everyone may suggest and discuss potential new
customs. This creates ownership and ensures the
rituals resonate with everybody engaged.

Consider frequency and simplicity: Choose
routines that match your family's schedule and
lifestyle. Weekly movie evenings are doable,
whereas lavish annual gatherings might not be
viable.

Incorporate symbolic elements: Use things that
link to the loved one's memories, such playing
their favorite music during gatherings or burning
candles with a specific aroma they adored.

Additional Tips:

Capture memories: Take photographs or films of your new customs to establish a visual record and revisit them in the future.

Share with extended family and friends: Invite people who knew the loved one to participate in your new customs, further enlarging the circle of remembering and consolation.

Embrace evolution: New traditions might grow over time. As your family grows and evolves, adjust them to keep their meaningfulness and create enduring memories.

Note:
Creating new traditions is not about deleting the past, but about weaving fresh strands of love and remembering into the present and future. By finding inspiration in your loved one's hobbies, developing important traditions, and incorporating everyone, you may construct a space where their memory lives on in a lively and joyful way. These new rituals become testaments to their effect, bringing solace and connection as your family journeys together, keeping their love in your hearts.

Remember:
Be age-appropriate: Adapt activities and talks to the developmental level and knowledge of each kid or teen.

Create a safe space: Encourage open communication and affirm all feelings, including sadness, anger, and bewilderment.

Seek expert help: If grieving feels overpowering or debilitating, don't hesitate to seek professional support from therapists or counselors specialized in grief and loss.

Additional Tips:
Involve children in designing events and traditions. This empowers them and develops a sense of responsibility in the mourning process.

Be flexible and adaptive. Allow space for individual wants and preferences inside the family.

Focus on the pleasant parts of remembering. Celebrate the life lived and the love shared, while acknowledging the grief of loss.

By implementing these recommendations into your journey of loss, this chapter helps you to convert the act of remembering into a source of healing, connection, and love. Remember, sorrow is a process, and honoring the memory of your loved one may be a beautiful and important part of that journey.

Chapter 6:

Finding Support: Navigating the Journey of Grief Together

Grief is a complex and intensely personal emotion, especially for adolescents, teenagers, and young adults. While navigating the raw emotions and digesting the loss might feel isolated, it's vital to understand you're not alone. Reaching out for and establishing support systems may be a critical step in healing and navigating this challenging road.
This chapter covers various support networks available and highlights their value in sharing the mourning experience with children, teenagers, and young adults.

1. Different Support Systems:

1. Family: A Complex Blend of Love and Support in Grief
Family, the cornerstone of many lives, provides enormous potential for both comfort and complication while managing sorrow. Let's look into the complicated dynamics at play:

Strengths of Family Support:
Familiarity and Security: The intrinsic tie between families, founded on shared history and affection, offers a sense of comfort and belonging. This sensation of "being understood" may be incredibly comforting amid emotional upheaval.

Unconditional Love and Acceptance: Ideally, family gives a space where emotions may be expressed openly, especially painful ones like sadness, without fear of condemnation. This acceptance acts as a solid pillar of emotional support.

Shared Memories and Rituals: Remembering the departed via shared tales, customs, and rituals promotes connection and helps keep their memory alive. This communal grieving process may be extremely healing for family members.

Practical Assistance: Beyond emotional support, family may give concrete aid with daily activities, financial obligations, or child care, easing practical tensions during a tough time.

Cultural Understanding: In many cultures, family plays a significant role in grieving rituals and customs, offering a structured framework for emotional expression and communal support.

Considerations and Navigating Challenges: Unresolved Issues: Existing family disputes or unresolved personal baggage might hamper good mourning and communication, sometimes aggravating grief instead of bringing relief.

Individual Differences: Grief emerges uniquely for each person. Family members may react in varied ways, leading to misunderstandings or disputes if empathy and open communication are missing.

Limited Emotional Capacity: Not all family members have the maturity, experience, or emotional bandwidth to help someone mourning properly. Some may battle with their own sorrow, seeking additional assistance themselves.

Communication Challenges: Family dynamics can make open communication difficult, leading to unstated expectations, cruel remarks, or inappropriate counsel. Setting clear limits and stating demands are vital to overcome these obstacles.

Cultural Dissonance: In certain families, cultural norms around grieving may contrast with individual needs or preferences, producing internal conflict and added stress. Finding a balance between honoring tradition and personal expression is vital.

Additional Points to Consider:
The quality and dynamics of family ties considerably determine the effectiveness of their assistance. Healthy, well-functioning families give enormous strength, while others may require external assistance.

Seeking professional aid alongside family support may be extremely valuable, offering extra direction and methods for coping.
It's appropriate to set limits with family members who struggle to give healthy support. Prioritize self-care and seek alternate sources of comfort if required.

Remember, forgiveness and empathy towards yourself and your family are crucial at this tough time.

By knowing both the strengths and limitations of family support, you may navigate this complicated area more successfully, gaining strength from the positive components while seeking extra resources when necessary. Remember, your well-being is vital, and prioritizing your emotional needs during this journey is crucial.

2. Friends: A Haven of Shared Understanding and Non-Judgmental Support

Beyond family, friends function as anchors in times of loss, bringing consolation and empathy on a road that might feel solitary. Here's a deeper look into the relevance and potential obstacles of obtaining support within your buddy circle:

Strengths of Friend Support:

Safe Space: Close friends establish a non-judgmental environment where you may openly share your feelings, worries, and anxieties without fear of condemnation. This free conversation enables for profound emotional release and affirmation.

Shared Experiences: Friends frequently share similar experiences, histories, or even losses, helping them to empathize with your grief on a personal level. This common knowledge builds empathy and creates a sense of not being alone on this arduous road.

Diverse viewpoints: Friends may give diverse viewpoints and coping techniques based on their experiences, broadening your arsenal for handling sorrow and finding what works best for you.

Distraction and Fun: Spending time with sympathetic friends may bring much-needed break from the intensity of mourning. Engaging in shared activities, laughing, and lighter moments can offer brief respite and remind you of life's delights.

Flexibility and Choice: Unlike family relationships, you may pick which friends to confide in based on their personality, level of comfort with sorrow, and your specific needs. This specialized help responds to your unique requirements.

Considerations and Navigating Challenges: Varying Levels of Comfort: Not all friends are skilled at handling intense emotions or possess the maturity to negotiate grieving successfully. Assess their personality and prior experiences to determine their readiness for emotional help.

Unintended counsel: Friends, however well-meaning, may provide counsel based on their own limited understanding of sorrow, thereby inflicting accidental damage or invalidating your feelings. Remember, emphasize communication and calmly explain your demands when negotiating such circumstances.

Limited Availability: Friends have their own lives and challenges. Respect their limitations and seek help from other sources if their availability or emotional capacity is constrained.

Friendship Dynamics: Existing conflict or unsolved difficulties within the buddy group might complicate obtaining help and generate additional stress. Choose companions that are emotionally mature and promote good communication.

Seeking Different Types of Support: Friends are vital, but they cannot meet every support requirement. Don't hesitate to seek professional treatment from therapists or join support groups for expert guidance and greater understanding.

Remember: Finding the correct pals for support is key. Choose people who are compassionate, supportive, and appreciative of your needs.

Open communication is crucial. Express your expectations and restrictions clearly to avoid misunderstandings.

Don't be hesitant to seek outside help if your friend group cannot satisfy all your needs.

Appreciate the role friends play in your recovery path, generating gratitude for their presence and understanding.

By managing these strengths and concerns, you may use the great importance of friends as a source of consolation and support during your mourning journey.

3. Therapists: Your Professional Guides on the Grief Journey
Grief, in its complexity, may sometimes overwhelm even the most supportive family and friends. In such circumstances, therapists emerge as beacons of expert counsel and support, strolling with you as you navigate the emotional landscape. Let's delve more into the relevance of treatment and the factors to navigate it effectively:

Strengths of Therapy:
Safe and Confidential Space: Therapists establish a non-judgmental and confidential setting where you may freely disclose your deepest feelings,

ideas, and weaknesses, knowing they are kept in safekeeping.

Professional Expertise: Trained in grief therapy and armed with evidence-based techniques, therapists understand the subtleties of grieving and hold many tools to help you process your emotions and establish healthy coping mechanisms.

Individualized Support: Unlike one-size-fits-all counsel, therapists customize their approach to your particular needs, considering your age, personality, and specific loss. This tailored attention offers relevant and effective support.

Validation and Understanding: Therapists actively listen and affirm your emotions, helping you negotiate complicated or overwhelming sensations without dismissing them as "unreasonable." This confirmation is vital for emotional recovery.
Trauma-Informed Care: When mourning originates from catastrophic loss, therapists educated in trauma-specific treatments can help you negotiate complicated emotions and manage post-traumatic stress symptoms successfully.

Developing Life Skills: Beyond immediate assistance, therapy prepares you with life skills like emotional control, communication, and self-care, helping you to cope with future obstacles and build resilience.

Considerations for Finding the Right Therapist: Finding the Right Fit: Not every therapist is a perfect match. Consider their specialty, demeanor, and communication style when picking someone you feel comfortable and understood by.

Cost and Insurance: Therapy can be pricey, although many therapists provide sliding-scale costs or take insurance. Explore possibilities and negotiate expenses upfront to guarantee affordability.

Active Participation: Therapy is a collaborative process. Your personal engagement, desire to open up, and dedication to using suggested skills are vital for its efficacy

Different Therapy Forms: Individual therapy gives concentrated assistance, while group therapy develops connection and shared experiences with those suffering similar losses. Explore several formats to find what suits you best.

Seeking Referrals: Ask reliable friends, family members, or healthcare experts for referrals. Utilize internet tools from respectable organizations like the American Psychological Association to focus your search.

Remember:
Therapy is not a sign of weakness but a significant investment in your mental and emotional well-being.

Don't hesitate to try different therapists until you discover the proper match. It's vital to feel comfortable and understood.

Therapy is a process, not a fast fix. Be gentle with yourself and trust the process.

Combining therapy with additional support systems like family, friends, or support groups can further enrich your healing path.

By receiving expert assistance and actively participating in therapy, you may gain vital help in negotiating the complexity of grieving, developing emotional healing, and enabling yourself to move on with more resilience.

4. Support Groups: A Collective Embrace in Shared Grief

Grief, albeit a very personal emotion, may feel solitary. In such circumstances, support groups arise as havens of shared understanding and solidarity, bringing solace and strength through collective experience. Let's examine the great importance of support groups and negotiate their intricacies for a genuinely fulfilling experience:

Strengths of Support Groups:

Validation and Shared Understanding: Hearing tales from people who have walked similar pathways validates your feelings and normalizes your experiences. Knowing you're not alone may be very reassuring and inspiring.

Peer Support and Belonging: Sharing your experience and building real connections with others develops a sense of belonging and community. This shared journey offers a secure environment for emotional expression and mutual support.

Diverse Insights and Learning: Sharing coping methods, tools, and experiences within the group enhances your toolkit for handling loss and gives fresh insights on your path.

Hope and Inspiration: Witnessing others manage their mourning journey with strength and resilience may offer hope and push you to go ahead on your own road.

Specific Grief Focus: Many groups focus on specific sorts of losses, such as child loss, marital loss, or pet loss. This tailored assistance allows you to connect with folks who understand the complexities of your unique grief.

Considerations for Finding the Right Group: Compatibility & Comfort: Not all groups are made equal. Choose one that corresponds with your age, personality, and unique needs. Ensure the group dynamic feels secure, supportive, and courteous.

Openness and Communication: Actively engage in conversations and share your experiences to obtain the best value. Remember, courteous communication and empathy are crucial.

Boundaries and Self-Care: Set boundaries as required and prioritize your emotional well-being. Don't feel pressured to discuss experiences that aren't comfortable yet.

Varied Formats: Explore online or in-person groups, closed or open groups, and groups with varied activity types to find what resonates with you.

Finding Support Groups: Utilize internet tools, community centers, religious organizations, or grief-specific websites to identify groups near you.

Remember:
Support groups are not a replacement for professional aid, but they may be a beneficial supplement to your entire support system.

It's good to "shop around" for a group that seems like the appropriate match. Don't hesitate to test several possibilities until you discover a community that resonates.

Respectful communication and empathy are key for getting the most of your support group experience.

Support groups may be a source of hope, inspiration, and connection on your grieving journey.

By actively engaging in a support group that matches with your needs and preferences, you may tap into the great power of shared experience, finding affirmation, consolation, and vital insights to traverse your grieving journey with empowered steps.

5. Online Resources: Navigating the Digital Seas of Support in Grief

The internet, generally perceived as a source of diversions, may surprisingly be a sanctuary for people navigating the turbulent waters of bereavement. Online services give knowledge, connection, and support, complementing traditional support systems and giving consolation for people who find physical interaction problematic. Let's delve deeper into the pros and considerations of this broad digital landscape:

Strengths of Online Resources:
Accessibility and Anonymity: Online services allow 24/7 access to information and help, breaking geographical and logistical constraints. Anonymity may be liberating for persons afraid to communicate openly in person.

Diversity of Resources: Websites, forums, blogs, and online support groups cater to various requirements, whether you're seeking for informative materials, peer-to-peer connection, or grief-specific tools and activities.

Specialized Support: Online platforms link you with groups enduring similar losses, such as miscarriage, pet loss, or addiction-related fatalities, giving tailored understanding and shared experiences.

Interactive Communities: Forums and online support groups give real-time interaction and support, building a sense of belonging and minimizing feelings of loneliness.

Knowledge Abundance: Credible websites and publications give in-depth knowledge about bereavement, coping processes, and mental health, helping you to understand your feelings and explore alternative healing approaches.
Considerations & Navigating Safely:
Credibility and Bias: Not all internet sources are created equal. Verify the author's competence and the website's repute before believing the information. Beware of biased or misleading content.

Privacy and Security: Protect your personal information and be wary of internet predators.

Utilize reliable websites and follow safety recommendations when interacting in online communities.

Overreliance and Isolation: While important, internet resources shouldn't replace real-world contacts and professional support. Seek a balance and prioritize face-to-face engagement where suitable.

Upsetting Anything: Be careful of your emotional state and avoid anything that might be upsetting or overpowering. Take pauses and emphasize your well-being.

Finding Quality Resources: Utilize trustworthy organizations like the National Alliance on Mental Illness (NAMI) or The Dougy Center, or ask healthcare experts for referrals.

Remember:
Online resources can be a helpful addition to your support system, including knowledge, connection, and strategies for coping.
Prioritize critical thinking and check facts before relying on it.

Use internet resources carefully, balancing them with offline relationships and expert aid.

Take care of your mental well-being and avoid excessive content.

By deliberately navigating the internet world, you may access a plethora of support and knowledge, allowing yourself to go ahead on your grieving journey with more clarity and connection.

2. The Importance of Support Systems:

Grief, in its multidimensional character, may leave us feeling adrift in a sea of overpowering emotions. It's during these stressful times that the necessity of support systems fully shines. These networks of care, established from family, friends, therapists, support groups, and even internet resources, give more than simply a helping hand; they become important pillars sustaining our emotional well-being as we negotiate the various pathways of grieving. Let's look further into the vital responsibilities these support systems play:

1. Validation and Understanding:
Breaking the Silence: Grief, with its kaleidoscope of emotions, may sometimes feel isolated. Sharing with supporting folks gives a secure environment to express the deepest sentiments,

from sadness and fury to uncertainty and guilt, without fear of condemnation. This confirmation normalizes your experience and reminds you that you're not alone in your quest.

Mirroring Your feelings: Supportive persons operate as mirrors, reflecting your feelings back to you in a way that develops comprehension. Recognizing the authenticity of your feelings – even the "messy" ones – brings enormous relief and removes the burden of self-doubt.

2. Sharing the Burden:
Lightening the Load: Grief, in its intensity, can feel like a heavy weight on your shoulders. Sharing your experiences with understanding folks helps you to shed part of that emotional weight, making the path a bit less onerous. Talking things out, sobbing together, or even sitting in quiet with someone who cares may provide a great sense of relief.

Distributing Responsibilities: Beyond emotional support, practical aid is vital during hard times. Whether it's sharing home duties, assisting with childcare, or running errands, support systems may ease practical responsibilities, allowing up room for you to focus on your emotional well-being.

3. Acquiring Coping Mechanisms:
Learning from Shared Experiences: No two grieving journeys are identical, yet everyone learns vital lessons along the way. Sharing methods and solutions that have benefited others might improve your coping toolkit. From mindfulness techniques and journaling to creative expression and interacting with nature, you may find what works best for you.

Discovering New Perspectives: Sometimes, the veil of loss can distort our judgment, making it difficult to perceive various methods of handling emotions. By listening to the experiences of those who have walked similar journeys, you can get fresh views and discover new coping techniques to overcome hard situations.

4. Fostering Hope and Connection:
Reminding You of Tomorrow: Grief may make it feel like the future is dreary and devoid of joy. Seeing the tenacity and optimism in others who have found their way through sorrow might

remind you that recovery is possible and that brighter days lay ahead. Their journeys act as beacons of hope, illuminating the route forward.

Combatting Isolation: The sense of being alone with your sadness may be devastating. Support networks create bridges, linking you to people who understand your sorrow. This sense of belonging develops emotional connection and combats the isolating character of grieving.

Beyond these critical tasks, support systems provide other benefits:

Encouragement and motivation: When the path becomes daunting, encouraging words and a little push from loved ones might be the fuel required to keep going forward.

Accountability and support: Sometimes, processing painful emotions or developing coping methods can be tricky. Supportive folks may hold you accountable and give encouragement, ensuring you continue on the path towards healing.

Celebrating milestones: As you advance through your grieving journey, celebrating even modest accomplishments with supportive folks generates

a sense of achievement and reinforces your
positive actions.

Remember:
Building a good support system requires time
and work. Don't hesitate to reach out to other
persons or investigate numerous resources to
discover a network that best matches your
requirements.

It's normal to have various expectations from
different support systems. Some may give
emotional understanding, while others might
provide practical aid.

Respect your own limitations and explain your
requirements properly to ensure you receive the
help that actually benefits you.

By developing a robust network of support, you
enable yourself to negotiate the various
pathways of loss with increased resilience,
understanding, and optimism. Remember, you
are not alone on this road; together, you can find
healing and move on towards a brighter future.

3. Engaging Children, Teens, and Young Adults in Grief: Building Bridges of Understanding and Support

Grief, with its complicated tapestry of emotions, may be particularly tough for children, teenagers, and young adults. Their emerging emotional frameworks and limited life experiences demand specific support systems that fit their individual needs. Let's investigate ways to effectively engage these age groups and give the assistance they need to handle grief:

1. Fostering Open Communication:
Creating a Safe Space: Children and young people frequently hesitate to share their emotions fearing judgment or burdening others. Create a safe atmosphere via open and honest interactions, telling them that there are no "right" or "wrong" sentiments.

Using Age-Appropriate Language: Simplify terminology and eliminate euphemisms that may mislead kids. Explain death using honest yet kind language, tailoring explanations to their developmental level and knowledge.
Active Listening: Truly listen without interrupting or providing unwanted advice. Validate their emotions and let them know you're there to simply listen and support them.

Utilizing Creative Expression: Encourage kids to express their thoughts through sketching, painting, writing, or simply playing - activities that may serve as emotional outlets and enhance communication.

2. Normalizing Their Emotions:
Validating All Feelings: It's vital to notice and affirm every feeling kids experience, from grief and rage to fear and guilt. Remind them that mourning is a natural response to loss, and these feelings are normal and anticipated.

Addressing Misconceptions: Correct any misunderstandings they may have about grieving, such as the assumption that melancholy implies they loved the person less, or that crying is a sign of weakness. Explain that there's no "right" way to grieve, and everyone experiences it differently.

Sharing Your Own Emotions: Let them know that you're mourning too, but in a way that doesn't dominate their experience. Sharing your feelings truthfully exhibits vulnerability and promotes a sense of shared understanding.

3. Adapting Support Systems to Their Needs:
Age-Appropriate Activities: Instead of typical talk therapy, try investigating art therapy, play therapy, or music therapy, which allow kids to express feelings via creative paths.

Peer Support Groups: Connecting with people their age who are enduring similar losses may give important support and a feeling of belonging. Explore age-specific grief support groups or programs in schools or community centers.

Family Rituals and customs: Involve them in establishing or preserving family rituals or customs in commemoration of the deceased. This can give a sense of comfort, connection, and continuity during tough circumstances.

Educational Resources: Age-appropriate books, websites, and videos can give vital knowledge on loss and different coping techniques. Guide them towards reputable materials that resonate with their interests and understanding.

4. Cultivating Patience and Understanding:
Acknowledging Individual Differences:
Remember, every kid, adolescent, and young adult grieves differently. Respect their particular

timeframes and avoid comparing their experience to others.

Accepting Setbacks: Healing isn't linear. There will be good days and bad days. Be patient and understanding when they regress or seem to take steps back in their emotional journey.

Celebrating tiny Victories: Acknowledge and appreciate even tiny victories along the road, like attending a support group meeting or expressing their feelings freely. Reinforce their development and perseverance.

Additional Tips:
Maintain routines and normalcy: As far as possible, keep to established habits and timetables, creating a feeling of security and familiarity during a hectic period.

Encourage self-care: Ensure they get adequate sleep, eat good foods, and engage in activities they like. Taking care of their physical and mental well-being is vital for recovery.

Seek expert assistance: If their loss feels overpowering or interferes with their everyday life, don't hesitate to seek professional support from a therapist or counselor specialized in child and teenage grieving.

By promoting open communication, normalizing emotions, modifying support networks, and giving tolerance and understanding, you may establish a bridge of support for children, teenagers, and young adults facing bereavement. Remember, your real presence, love, and wisdom may make a world of difference in their recovery process.

Remember, finding the correct support system is vital. Experiment with several possibilities and determine what feels most comfortable and useful for you and your loved ones. Seeking professional aid is always suggested if required.

This chapter provides a starting point for understanding diverse support networks and their relevance in handling sorrow. By cultivating open conversation, getting appropriate help, and being patient with yourself and your loved ones, you may journey through sorrow and find healing together.

Chapter 7:

Growing Through Loss: Shifting the Focus to Personal Growth and Resilience

Loss is a universal feeling, but for children, teenagers, and young adults, it may be extremely tough. While the agony of loss is apparent, it's crucial to remember that even despite mourning, personal development and resilience are possible. Shifting the focus towards these good outcomes helps allow young people to navigate their grieving journey in a productive way.

Before discussing development and resilience, realizing the consequences of loss is vital. Young kids may experience a range of emotions, including grief, anger, uncertainty, and fear. They may retreat from activities they formerly loved, have difficulty focusing, or feel physical symptoms like exhaustion or changes in appetite.

Recognizing these emotions as natural and accepting their feelings is vital to providing a safe environment for recovery.

While grieving, it's normal to fixate on the unpleasant elements of loss. However, supporting young people to redirect their attention towards development and resilience can empower them to discover purpose and strength in their experiences. Here are some crucial issues to discuss:

1. Personal Growth: Discussing Growth through Loss: Elaborating on Skill Development

Here's how you might elaborately describe the abilities young people learn after loss, concentrating on resilience, independence, and empathy, using many examples:

Resilience:
Highlight particular situations: Talk about particular problems they faced and how they overcame them. Did they face difficulties but persisted? Did they discover inventive answers in difficult times?

Focus on emotional regulation: Did they develop new coping skills for tough emotions, such writing, breathing exercises, or seeking support? Did they display self-compassion during hard moments?

Celebrate their determination: Point out occasions they demonstrated endurance and strength. Did they continue with activities despite grief or difficulty? Did they face their concerns and take fresh moves forward?

Examples:
"Remember when you felt overwhelmed after the loss, but you talked to a friend and learned new methods to handle your sadness? That displays incredible resilience!"

"It was remarkable how you maintained your dance lesson even when you felt bad. That requires significant strength and dedication."

"Facing your phobia of public speaking even if you missed your loved one at the occasion was incredibly gutsy. That's the spirit of resiliency!"

Independence:
Discuss growing responsibility: Did they take on additional chores around the house or become more self-sufficient in daily activities?

Emphasize problem-solving abilities: Did they tackle difficulties independently or find inventive answers to challenges?

Celebrate their resourcefulness: Did they learn to manage new circumstances without constantly depending on others?

Examples:
"Taking up preparing dinner for the family is a tremendous duty, and you've been doing it magnificently following the loss. You're growing more autonomous!"

"I watched how you worked out how to utilize the new library system on your own. That displays strong problem-solving skills and independence."

"It's remarkable how you managed to tackle that challenging circumstance at school by yourself. You're getting more resourceful and confident."

Empathy:
Share instances of compassion: Did they provide assistance to those who were mourning or suffering challenges? Did they demonstrate empathy and compassion towards others' emotions?

Highlight active listening: Did they listen closely to others' feelings and give emotional support?

Connect empathy to social skills: Did their empathy enhance their connections and interactions with others?

Examples:
"The way you comforted your buddy who lost their cat was very kind and empathic. You actually comprehend what they're going through."

"I admire how you listened carefully to your sibling and provided words of encouragement. You're a fantastic listener and friend."

"Your sensitivity shows through when you engage with people. It makes you a compassionate and supportive person, which will benefit you and your relationships."

Remember to:
Tailor your examples to the individual's personal experiences.

Use encouraging and uplifting words.

Celebrate their unique path and progress.

Offer hope and encouragement for the future.

By addressing these abilities and offering real examples, you may help young people see the good results of their experiences and embrace their personal growth through loss.

This can help their general well-being and equip them to confront future obstacles with confidence.

Identifying New Opportunities: Blossoming after Loss:
Loss may provide doors to new experiences and self-discovery. Encourage them to investigate topics they may have put off or discover new interests.

While loss may be a tremendously painful experience, it can also act as a catalyst for personal growth and discovery. By encouraging young people to seek new options, you may help them find meaning and purpose amongst their sadness. Here are various methods to debate and expound on this concept:

1. Uncovering Hidden Passions:
Ask contemplative questions: Encourage them to ponder about things they've always wanted to attempt but put off. What activities inspired their

curiosity in the past? Are there pastimes they've admired from afar?

Connect loss to self-discovery: Discuss how loss may sometimes lead to a rethink of priorities and values. Encourage them to pursue activities that correspond with their newfound sense of self.

Share inspiring stories: Talk about individuals who developed new passions after overcoming hardships. This might give hope and drive for their own exploration.

Example: "Remember how you always wanted to play guitar but never had time? Maybe this is the right chance to pursue that interest. It might be a terrific method to express your feelings and connect with your inner musician."

2. Expanding Horizons: Suggest new experiences: Introduce them to activities beyond their comfort zone, including volunteering, joining a group, or taking a class in a new topic.

Emphasize the learning aspect: Frame new encounters as chances to learn and develop, not merely fill a need.

Offer support and encouragement: Be their cheerleader and assist them manage any hurdles they experience in their adventure.

Example: "Have you considered volunteering at an animal shelter? It might be a meaningful way to interact with animals while benefiting others. It's also an opportunity to meet new people who share your enthusiasm."

3. Redefining ties: Encourage deeper connections: Loss can sometimes lead to a yearning for better ties. Encourage them to reconnect with old acquaintances, develop new relationships, or deepen current ones.

Explore new communities: Suggest joining organizations, groups, or online communities based on common interests or principles. This might create a sense of belonging and support.

Highlight the importance of social connection: Discuss how meaningful connections may help to healing and general well-being.

Example: "Remember how you expressed wanting to meet others who share your love for art? Maybe joining the local art group would be a terrific opportunity to meet with like-minded folks and pursue your interest further."

Remember:
Be patient and understanding: Allow them time and space to explore and discover what resonates with them.

Celebrate their efforts: Acknowledge and praise their willingness to venture outside their comfort zone.

Focus on the positive: Emphasize the personal growth and delight that may come from new experiences.

By encouraging young people to seek new options, you may help them find meaning and purpose beyond their loss. This can enable children to embrace growth, create resilience, and construct a brighter future.

Celebrate their strengths:
Remind them of their unique talents and strengths that can help them overcome obstacles.

Celebrating Strengths: Building Confidence in the Face of Loss

Loss may leave young people feeling vulnerable and unsure of themselves. However, reminding kids of their particular qualities may be a valuable tool for promoting confidence and resilience. Here are some methods to discuss and elaborate on recognizing their strengths:

1. Identify Unique Qualities:

Focus on individual strengths: Instead of general comments, highlight their individual abilities, personality traits, or skills. Do they have a good sense of humor, are they innovative problem-solvers, or do they exhibit steadfast kindness?

Connect strengths to prior experiences: Share concrete occasions where their strengths helped them overcome hurdles or achieve their goals. This personalizes the compliment and encourages their strengths.

Example:

"Remember when you utilized your humor to lighten the mood during that stressful family gathering? Your ability to make others laugh is a great skill that can help you handle any problem."

2. Encourage Self-Reflection:
Guide them in finding their strengths: Ask
open-ended questions that enable them to think
on their good characteristics and talents. What
do they love doing? What are they excellent at?
What makes them proud of themselves?

Validate their self-assessment: Acknowledge and
applaud the strengths they identify, even if they
seem minor or unnoticed.
Example:
"You remarked that you're skilled at listening to
people and giving help. That's a significant
strength, because it indicates you have a kind
and sensitive heart."

3. Connect Strengths to Future Growth: Show
how strengths might assist overcome future
challenges: Discuss how their talents might serve
as tools for managing future hurdles and
accomplishing their goals.

Promote self-belief: Encourage them to trust in
their abilities to overcome problems and accept
new chances, using their strengths as their
compass.
Example:
"Your inventiveness helped you develop
innovative solutions throughout this challenging

moment. Remember that when you encounter future obstacles, your creative thinking will be a tremendous tool."

4. Celebrate Effort and Progress: Don't simply focus on achievements: Recognize and appreciate their work and development, even if they haven't accomplished their ultimate objective. This develops a development mentality and encourages perseverance.

Highlight little victories: Acknowledge and applaud even tiny steps people take towards recovery or personal improvement. This encourages favorable habits and promotes confidence.

Example: "I know it's been challenging, but I'm really proud of you for trying that new activity. Taking that move demonstrates your courage and willingness to improve, which are great qualities."

Remember:
Be sincere and specific: Avoid generic compliments and focus on their individual talents.

Tailor your approach to their age and personality.

Celebrate their strengths frequently and truthfully.

Focus on the positive influence of their strengths.

By celebrating their strengths, you may help young people create a good self-image, establish confidence, and discover the fortitude to confront obstacles and embrace progress, even in the face of loss. This may be a powerful step in their path of healing and resilience.

2. Building Resilience: Equipping Young Minds with Healthy Coping Mechanisms

Explore relaxation techniques, mindfulness exercises, journaling, or creative outlets as strategies to manage challenging emotions. Loss may spark a range of challenging emotions, leaving young people feeling overwhelmed and unsure how to deal. By researching and practicing healthy coping techniques, individuals can acquire the resilience needed to manage their loss and emerge stronger. Here's how you might talk and expound on creating resilience:

1. Exploring a Toolbox of Coping Mechanisms:
Introduce varied options: Don't limit yourself to a
particular technique. Offer a choice of
possibilities, such as:

Relaxation techniques: Deep breathing exercises,
gradual muscular relaxation, guided visualization.

Mindfulness practices: Meditation, mindful walks,
focussing on the present moment.

Creative outlets: Journaling, sketching, painting,
performing music.

Physical activity: Exercise, yoga, dancing,
spending time in nature.

Social connection: Talking to trusted friends,
family, or therapists.

2. Matching Mechanisms to Individual Needs:
Emphasize self-awareness: Encourage young
people to determine what works best for them.
What relaxes their mind? What helps them
communicate their emotions?

Experimentation is key: Encourage them to try
different tactics and see what resonates. Their
demands and tastes may alter throughout time.

Tailor the approach: Consider their age, personality, and cultural background when proposing coping techniques.

3. Providing Specific Examples:
Share personal experiences: If you've found a specific approach beneficial, share it truthfully, stressing how it helped you handle unpleasant emotions.

Offer resources: Provide age-appropriate literature, websites, or applications that give advice on various coping techniques.

Connect to relevant stories: Share tales of those who have utilized certain approaches to overcome obstacles.

Example:
"Remember when you felt overwhelmed after a quarrel with your friend? Taking those deep breaths helped you calm down and convey your thoughts more clearly. Deep breathing may be a helpful strategy if you feel anxious."

4. Integrating Coping Mechanisms into Daily Life:
Encourage frequent practice: Suggest
implementing preferred coping methods into
their daily routine, even when they don't feel
overwhelmed.

Make it enjoyable and engaging: Find methods to
make exercising coping techniques pleasant,
such as converting writing into creative
storytelling or mixing mindfulness with nature
hikes.

Celebrate their efforts: Acknowledge and applaud
their desire to explore new coping techniques
and build resilience.

5. Seeking Professional Support:
Normalize requesting help: Remind them that
professional therapists may give further
assistance and advice in building coping
techniques.

Offer resources: Help them discover
age-appropriate therapists or counselors
specialized in sorrow and loss.

Emphasize the benefits: Frame obtaining
professional treatment as a means to invest in
their well-being and emotional growth.

Remember:
Be patient and understanding: Building resilience
requires time and effort.

Focus on empowering them, not prescribing
answers.

Celebrate their progress, no matter how modest.

Be a trusted source of support and
encouragement.

By discovering and practicing healthy coping
techniques, young people may acquire the
resilience they need to manage tough emotions,
recover from loss, and emerge stronger and
more confident individuals.

Emphasizing the Importance of Support: Building
a Network of Strength
Encourage them to connect with supportive
friends, family members, or therapists who may
give understanding and encouragement.

Loss may frequently isolate young people,
leaving them to feel alone and misunderstood.
By highlighting the value of support, you may
urge them to connect with people who can give

empathy, encouragement, and a feeling of belonging during their challenging journey. Here are some methods to explore and expound on this key part of building resilience:

1. Identifying Different Sources of Support:
Family and friends: Highlight the value of interacting with trusted family members and friends who give non-judgmental listening ears and emotional support. Discuss how sharing their feelings with loved ones may give comfort and understanding.

Peer support groups: Encourage researching support groups particularly tailored for young people suffering a loss. Sharing experiences with others who understand their problems may be very affirming and inspiring.

Grief counselors or therapists: Emphasize the benefits of receiving professional treatment from therapists specialized in grieving and loss. These specialists can offer guided exploration of emotions, coping techniques, and healthy processing of the loss.
2. Matching Needs to the Right Support System:
Consider their personality and preferences: Some individuals may find peace in confiding in close friends, while others may prefer expert counsel.

Encourage them to pick the support system that seems most comfortable and beneficial.

Respect their boundaries: Not everyone requires the same degree of help. Respect their desire for privacy or space while gently urging them to connect when they are ready.

Offer resources and assistance: Help them discover appropriate support groups, therapists, or online communities based on their individual needs and interests.

3. Framing Support as a Strength, Not a Weakness: Challenge the stigma around requesting help: Dispel the misunderstanding that requesting help is a sign of weakness. Reinforce that asking for help is a show of strength and courage, especially during hard circumstances.

Share uplifting stories: Share stories of folks who have benefited from reaching out for help after facing loss. This can indicate the good influence of connecting with people.

Normalize getting professional help: Emphasize that therapists are there to advise and help, not judge. Normalize obtaining professional treatment as a method to invest in their well-being and emotional growth.

4. Actively Engage and Encourage Sharing: Start conversations: Initiate open and honest talks about their thoughts and experiences.
Let them know they have a safe area to express themselves without judgment.

Actively listen: When they share, provide your complete attention and listen without interrupting. Validate their emotions and recognize their anguish.

Offer practical help: Beyond emotional support, offer actual assistance with everyday duties or errands that may feel overwhelming during this time. This might display your caring and ease further tension.

5. Celebrating Connections and Progress: Acknowledge their efforts: Recognize and applaud their willingness to reach out for help. This might drive them to continue creating and maintaining their support network.

Highlight the advantages of connection: Share good parts of their contacts with supporting folks, including how it offered them comfort or helped them develop new insights.

Promote self-advocacy: Encourage them to be aggressive in their needs and talk freely with their support system about what they find useful.

Remember:
Be patient and understanding: Building trust and connecting with others requires time and effort. Respect their pace and encourage them to open out gradually.

Lead by example: Show them the significance of support by being a trustworthy source of encouragement and listening to yourself.

Focus on enabling people, not managing their connections.

Celebrate their progress, no matter how modest.

By highlighting the value of support and helping young people connect with folks who care, you may establish a powerful safety net that helps them to navigate their grieving journey with more resilience and find peace at tough moments.

Reframe challenges as chances: Help them perceive challenges as opportunities to learn and grow, highlighting the strength obtained from conquering hurdles.

Reframing Challenges as Opportunities: Fostering Growth via Obstacles
Loss may bring great obstacles, leaving young people feeling disillusioned and depressed. However, reframing these problems as chances for learning and growth can enable individuals to find their resilience and emerge stronger. Here's how you may help kids perceive problems as stepping stones to personal development:

1. Shifting Perspective:
Challenge negative self-talk: Encourage them to detect and combat negative beliefs like "I can't handle this" or "This is too hard." Help them reframe these ideas into possibilities for progress, such as "This is challenging, but I can learn from it and become stronger."
Focus on the broader picture: Remind them that problems are transient and part of life's journey. Encourage them to see them as chances to acquire vital skills and resilience that will benefit them in the long term.

Connect to relevant stories: Share stories of individuals who have overcome enormous problems and transformed them into opportunities for growth and good change.

2. Identifying the Learning Potential: Discuss hidden lessons: Ask them what they can learn from the issues they're encountering. Are there new abilities they can learn, like problem-solving or controlling emotions? Can they learn more about themselves and their strengths?

Focus on transferable skills: Highlight how the abilities they receive from conquering problems may be applied to other aspects of their life, such academics, relationships, or future employment.

Celebrate minor victories: Encourage children to identify even modest measures of growth as crucial lessons and signs of their rising strength.

3. Emphasizing Personal Growth: Connect obstacles to personal values: Encourage them to think on how conquering problems might help them live according to their values, such persistence, courage, or compassion.

Celebrate improved self-awareness: Discuss how experiencing problems may lead to a deeper understanding of themselves, their strengths, and their capacity to manage with hardship.

Promote growth attitude: Encourage them to adopt a growth mindset, thinking that their talents may develop and improve through work and determination.

4. Building Confidence via Overcoming Obstacles:
Celebrate their efforts: Recognize and praise their willingness to tackle obstacles and put in the work to overcome them. This encourages their confidence and inspires them to persist.

Highlight their strengths: Remind them of the strengths they've utilized to overcome prior problems. This creates confidence and encourages them to approach new hurdles with a positive attitude.

Connect challenges to future aspirations: Discuss how conquering present problems might prepare them for reaching their future goals and desires. This creates a sense of purpose and motivation.

5. Seeking Support and Sharing Experiences:
Encourage reaching out: Remind them that they don't have to confront issues alone. Encourage them to seek help from reliable friends, family, or therapists who can give direction and encouragement.

Sharing may be empowering: Facilitate conversations where people can share their experiences and problems with others. This may be a wonderful method to learn from each other's viewpoints and acquire insight.

Promote good coping methods: Encourage them to continue practicing healthy coping mechanisms like relaxation techniques, mindfulness practices, or journaling to manage stress and emotions during hard times.

Remember:
Be patient and understanding: Reframing difficulties takes time and experience. Don't urge them to see things differently overnight.

Focus on empowerment, not control: Guide them to develop their own viewpoints and strengths, not imposing your own.

Celebrate their progress, no matter how modest.

Be a trusted source of support and
encouragement.

By helping young people reframe obstacles as
opportunities for growth, you may encourage
them to develop a positive attitude, build
resilience, and emerge stronger and more
confident individuals, equipped to manage life's
complexity with wisdom and bravery.

3. Maintaining Connection: Honoring Loved Ones Through Positive Memories

Share pleasant memories: Encourage them to
keep the memory of their loved one alive by
sharing tales, reminiscing, or engaging in
activities they liked together.

Loss, while very painful, doesn't have to
obliterate the love and connection experienced
with the loved one. By encouraging young people
to share pleasant memories, reminisce, and
engage in activities they liked together, you may
help them keep a valued connection and honor
the life of their loved one. Here's how to explain
and expound on this key component of healing:

1. Fostering Openness and Comfort:

Create a safe space: Let them know it's alright to talk about their loved one, even if it conjures up emotions. Offer your presence and listening ear without judgment.

Validate their feelings: Acknowledge the sadness of loss but also encourage them to share happy memories and tales they appreciate.

Offer varied options: Suggest several methods to interact with memories, such as chatting, writing, building a memory box, or visiting memorable places.

2. Sharing Stories and Reminiscing:
Encourage storytelling: Ask them to share tales about their loved one, their personalities, idiosyncrasies, and humorous situations. Encourage them to involve others in these talks.

Look through images and keepsakes: Review old photographs, letters, or other memorabilia together. Reflect on the wonderful emotions and memories they inspire.

Create digital memories: Help them create digital scrapbooks, slideshows, or recordings of tales to preserve memories in a new manner.

3. Engaging in Shared Activities:
Continue traditions: If their loved one enjoyed specific activities, urge them to continue them, either alone or with others who shared the experience.

Visit cherished places: Spend time in sites significant to their loved one, such as their favorite park, restaurant, or vacation area. Share recollections and reflect on their particular friendship.

Engage in pastimes they enjoyed: If their loved one had a specific activity, urge them to attempt it themselves or share it with others who might like it.

4. Finding Meaning and Purpose:
Connect memories to values: Help them identify values their loved one embodied, such compassion, humor, or inventiveness. Encourage adopting these principles into their own life.

Engage in volunteer work: Find volunteer opportunities connected to their loved one's hobbies or issues they supported. This may be a meaningful way to respect their memory and connect with others.

Create something in their honor: Encourage them to create a song, poetry, or tale inspired by their loved one, or plant a tree in their memory.

5. Celebrating Life, not Just Loss:
Focus on the positive influence: Encourage them to focus on the good impact their loved one had on their life and the lives of others. Celebrate the pleasure and love they shared.

Create rituals of remembrance: Establish regular rituals to memorialize their loved one, such lighting a candle on their birthday or sharing recollections on their anniversary.

Remember, love never dies: Emphasize that while the physical presence is gone, the love and connection remain. Encourage them to take that love forward in their own lives.

Note: Be patient and understanding: Healing takes time, and there's no right or wrong way to grieve. Respect their individual process.

Offer help and guidance: Be a solid source of support and make advice when required, but don't press them into things they're not ready for.

Focus on allowing them to establish their own unique manner of remembering their loved one.

Celebrate their attempts to maintain connection, no matter how tiny.

By encouraging young people to share happy memories and engage in activities that remember their loved one, you may help them preserve a valued connection, find meaning in their loss, and celebrate the life that impacted theirs so intimately.

Maintaining Connection: Honoring Loved Ones Through Positive Memories (Comprehensively) Suggest constructing a monument, helping in a cause their loved one cared about, or initiating a habit that respects their memory.
Loss can leave a gaping hole, but the love and connection shared with a loved one don't have to evaporate totally. By encouraging young people to actively interact with happy memories, you may help them preserve a meaningful connection, celebrate the life of their loved one, and nurture healing in the process. Here's a full study of this key component of grief:

1. Creating a Safe and Open Space:
Normalize emotional expression: Let them know it's totally appropriate to feel sad, angry, perplexed, or any other feeling that emerges. Offer a judgment-free environment to discuss honestly about their loved one and their feelings.

Validate their experience: Acknowledge the sadness they're experiencing, but also urge them to embrace the wonderful emotions linked with their loved one's memories.

Respect individual preferences: Understand that everyone grieves differently. Offer numerous opportunities for connecting with memories, respecting their comfort level and speed.

2. Fostering Remembrance via Sharing and Reflection:
Encourage storytelling: Invite them to share humorous tales, meaningful experiences, or even ordinary routines they enjoyed with their loved one. Encourage them to share these experiences with people who knew and loved the individual.

Create a memory box or scrapbook: Collect photographs, notes, souvenirs, and other physical memories of their loved one. Dedicate time to reminiscing together, thinking on the emotions and tales linked with each object.

Use technology to preserve memories: Help them make digital albums, slideshows, or recordings of their stories. This may be a great technique to preserve memories for future generations and revisit them quickly.

3. Engaging in Shared Activities and Traditions:
Continue significant traditions: If their loved one cherished certain hobbies or rituals, urge them to keep them alive. This might be anything from creating a birthday cake to visiting their favorite park or participating in a community event they sponsored.

Seek out shared spaces: Spend time in areas that carried great meaning for their loved one, such as their favorite restaurant, vacation site, or childhood home. Reflect on the memories linked with these places and enhance the emotional connection.

Explore their loved one's interests: If their loved one had a specific activity or passion, attempt it yourself or urge them to share it with others who might enjoy it. This might be a method to connect with their memory and learn more about them.

4. Finding Purpose and Meaning in Their Loss:
Connect memories to values: Help them identify the values their loved one exemplified, such compassion, humor, or tenacity. Encourage children to apply these principles into their own lives and activities, passing their heritage forward.

Engage in volunteer work: Find volunteer opportunities connected to their loved one's hobbies or issues they supported. This might be a meaningful way to respect their memory and connect with others who share similar ideals.

Create something in their honor: Encourage them to create a poem, song, tale, or simply draw a picture inspired by their loved one. This may be a method to convey their sentiments, honor their memory, and leave a lasting monument.

5. Celebrating Life and Nurturing the Bond:
Focus on the positive impact: Encourage them to focus on the pleasure, laughter, and love their loved one brought into their life and the lives of

others. Celebrate the wonderful effect they made and the memories they produced.

Create rituals of remembrance: Establish regular rituals to memorialize their loved one, such as lighting a candle on their birthday, visiting their cemetery on their anniversary, or exchanging tales on their special days. These rituals can bring comfort and enhance the bond over time.

Remember, love never dies: Remind them that while the physical presence is gone, the love and connection they enjoyed with their loved one remain. Encourage them to carry that love forward in their own lives, respecting their legacy in their actions and decisions.

Beyond these precise topics, here are some other considerations:

Age and developmental level: Tailor your approach to the young person's age and comprehension of death and grief. Use age-appropriate terminology and activities.

Cultural and religious beliefs: Be conscious of cultural and religious traditions around death and grief, and respect individual rituals and beliefs.

Professional help: Encourage getting professional support from therapists or grief counselors who specialize in working with young people.

Patience and understanding: Remember, healing is a unique and individual process. Be patient with their pace and give support and understanding throughout their journey.

By establishing a safe environment for sharing memories, promoting meaningful involvement, and honoring the life of their loved one, you may assist young people negotiate the complicated feelings of loss and retain a treasured connection that transcends the physical absence. Remember, your support and wisdom may be crucial at this tough time.

Remember:
Individual pace: Healing isn't linear. Each person grieves at their own speed and in their own way. Avoid encouraging young people to move on too early.

Seek professional help: If grieving is overpowering or disrupting everyday life, advocate obtaining professional treatment from a therapist or counselor specialized in grief and loss.

By addressing the effects of loss while stressing
personal growth and resilience, you may enable
young people to manage their grieving journey in
a healthy and productive way. Remember,
recovery takes time, and your support and
direction may make a major impact in their life.

PART THREE:

The Path Forward

The road of mourning, especially for children, teenagers, and young adults, is frequently riddled with ambiguity and anguish. While the first shock dissipates, the waves of grief and loss might continue to ebb and flow, leaving one feeling adrift. Yet, within the gloom, there glimmers of optimism waiting to be uncovered. In this final part, we go on a journey of learning and acceptance. We discuss the truth that healing takes time, with ups and downs that are a natural part of the process.

We dive into the topic of hope, reminding us that pleasure and laughter may still flourish despite the tears. Finally, we stand together, united in the knowledge that you are not alone.

This section includes practical ideas for handling difficult days, links for further help, and a message of steadfast optimism and unity.

Chapter 8: Healing Takes Time - A Gentle Journey Through Ups and Downs:

This chapter acts as a warm hand on your shoulder, encouraging you that mending isn't a linear sprint, but a prolonged climb with unavoidable ups and downs. It goes into the normality of these oscillations, reminding you that terrible days are part of the process. Practical advice and tactics are presented, such as writing, expressing feelings via art, and seeking assistance from loved ones, to traverse these challenging situations with grace and understanding. Remember, healing isn't about removing the pain; it's about learning to live with it in a way that allows you to breathe and develop.

Chapter 9: Hope and New Beginnings - Finding Joy in the Midst of Grief:
This chapter introduces the transformational power of hope. It acknowledges the apparently hard job of finding joy again, but softly reminds you that laughter and brightness may still exist alongside sorrow. It discusses techniques to nurture hope, such as cherishing memories, discovering beauty in the world around you, and focusing on the simple things that offer you peace. It encourages you to welcome new experiences and create new memories, not as substitutes, but as adds to the fabric of your life. Remember, hope isn't about ignoring the past;

it's about embracing the future with a feeling of possibilities.

Chapter 10: You Are Not Alone - A Beacon of Solidarity and Support:
This chapter shines as a light of solidarity, reminding you that you are not navigating this route alone. It acknowledges the sensation of isolation that sorrow may cause, but gives a powerful message: you are surrounded by a network of support. It gives tools and channels to connect with people who understand your path, whether through support groups, internet forums, or professional treatment. Remember, sharing your sadness may be a source of enormous strength and consolation. You are not alone; together, we can travel this journey.This part extends beyond the websites, delivering a complete collection of resources geared to different age groups and needs. It includes hotlines, websites, and publications particularly designed to help children, teenagers, and young adults through their grieving journey.

Remember, getting professional help is a show of strength, not weakness. There are individuals who care and want to assist you navigate this tough time.Remember, sorrow is a unique and personal experience. There is no right or incorrect way to approach it. This section is your caring guide, giving practical tools, words of encouragement, and a network of support. As you pursue your own route forward, realize that you are not alone. There is hope, there is light, and there is a future waiting for you. Take each step with confidence, and remember, you are stronger than you believe.

Chapter 8:

Healing Takes Time: A Compassionate Guide for Young Hearts

Imagine a river running slowly, sometimes surging over rapids, sometimes meandering over tranquil areas. This is how healing works. It's a journey, not a destination, with its own rhythm of ups and downs. This chapter is here to help you through those waters, giving comfort, support, and practical resources to manage the challenging days.

1. Navigating the Emotional Spectrum: It's Okay to Feel Everything

Grief creates a vibrant canvas of feelings, a kaleidoscope of loss, rage, uncertainty, numbness, and occasionally, even joy. It's vital to realize that any color in this palette is legitimate. There's no right or wrong way to grieve, no one road to follow. You take this path at your own speed, feeling whatever feelings occur.

Let's investigate some of these frequent emotions:

Sadness: This overpowering emptiness, desire, and sorrow is a natural reaction to loss. Allow yourself to weep, express your pain, and seek consolation in support networks.

Anger: It's natural to feel furious at the injustice of the situation, at the world, or even at your loved one who is gone. Acknowledge your anger, express it appropriately (through exercise, writing, or talking to a trusted friend), and don't let it overtake you.

Confusion: The world could feel upside down following a loss. It's acceptable to feel puzzled, doubting all you know. Give yourself time to analyze and comprehend your feelings, seeking help from people who can give insight.

Numbness: Sometimes, the agony is so overpowering that we shut off emotionally. This numbness is a coping technique, but it's crucial not to stay stuck there. Gently guide yourself back into emotion, getting expert treatment if needed.

Delight: It can sound unusual, but experiencing
moments of delight despite mourning is totally
natural. Sharing a good memory, laughing with
loved ones, or discovering beauty in nature
doesn't decrease your love for the one you lost.
Embrace these experiences as testaments to the
life you shared.

Remember:
You're not alone. Everyone grieves differently,
yet numerous others have walked this route
before you. Seek help from friends, family,
therapists, or support groups who may give
understanding and comfort.

Be gentle to yourself. This is a marathon, not a
sprint. Be patient with your growth, recognize
even minor successes, and treat yourself with
care.

Talk it out. Bottling up emotions may be
hazardous. Find a safe area to express your
feelings, whether it's through writing, talking to a
therapist, or confiding in a trusted friend.

This process of grieving is unique to you. Accept
your feelings, accept the support of loved ones,
and remember, you are stronger than you
believe. Every cry, every laugh, every stride

forward portrays a picture of your strength and
your ability to recover.

Healing isn't linear:
Healing's Winding Road: Embrace the Ups and
Downs

Grief's path isn't a smooth, upward trek. It's a
twisting path with unforeseen twists and turns,
good days drenched in sunshine, and dismal
valleys covered in fog. Remember: recovery isn't
linear, and that's alright.

Imagine: You're hiking this trail. Sometimes, you
reach a stunning sight, feeling lighter and
hopeful. On other days, the fog sets in, and you
stumble back, disoriented and disappointed.
Don't confuse these setbacks for retreat. They're
simply part of the terrain.

Here's why anticipating a straight line is
unrealistic:

Memories arrive in waves.
You can be cheerfully going about your day when
a sudden surge of remembrance floods over you,
bringing back the anguish of loss. This doesn't
imply you're regressing; it's just your brain
processing.

Triggers lurk behind corners.
Anniversaries, familiar tunes, even fragrances
might unexpectedly provoke floods of
melancholy. These reactions are natural, not
setbacks. Be cognizant of your triggers and have
coping techniques in place.

Growth isn't always evident. Healing happens in
unseen ways too. Maybe you're able to talk
about your loved one without breaking down, or
perhaps you can partake in activities you used to
find difficult. These are signals of growth, even if
they feel subtle.

So, how do you manage this rough terrain?

Embrace the rollercoaster.
Accept that happy days and unpleasant days are
both inevitable. Don't criticize yourself for feeling
unhappy; instead, accept your feelings and let
them flow.

Celebrate minor successes.
Did you get out of bed today? Did you chat to a
friend? These apparently modest steps are
testaments to your strength and endurance.

Be patient with yourself.
Healing takes time, sometimes a lot of it. Be nice
to yourself, exercise self-compassion, and
understand that growth isn't always linear.

Seek help.
When the path gets too tough, don't hesitate to
depend on loved ones, therapists, or support
groups. Sharing your story with others can
alleviate the strain and give useful insight.

Healing is a twisting route, but you don't have to
walk it alone. Remember, even when the fog
settles, the sun will ultimately burst through.
Embrace the trip, trust the process, and know
that you have the strength to traverse it, one
step at a time.

You're not alone:
Grief may feel isolated, like you're the only one
afloat in a sea of sadness. But remember, this
isn't your truth. Countless people have walked
this journey before you, and many are traveling
it with you right now. Reaching out for help is
vital, not a show of weakness, but a tribute to
your courage and commitment to recover.

Here are several safe havens you may navigate to:

Family and friends: They may not entirely comprehend your suffering, but their love and presence can be important. Share your story, weep together, or simply sit in comfortable quiet. Don't hesitate to ask for particular types of assistance, whether it's a listening ear, help with errands, or a shoulder to weep on.

Therapists or counselors: Trained experts can give a safe space to express your emotions without judgment and provide support for managing your sorrow. They can also equip you with appropriate coping techniques and help you manage difficult feelings.

Support groups: Connecting with people who understand your loss may be immensely affirming and reassuring. Sharing your experiences and finding consolation in their adventures may generate a feeling of camaraderie and belonging. Online or in-person, support groups offer a tremendous network of empathy and understanding.

Remember:
Talking is therapeutic. Bottling up your feelings might be hazardous. Finding someone you trust to listen, whether it's a loved one, therapist, or support group member, may give enormous comfort and insight.

Support comes in various kinds. It doesn't have to be long, drawn-out chats. Sharing a joke with a buddy, attending a grief-focused event, or simply having someone check in on you may all be forms of helpful connection.

You deserve to be heard. Your voice counts, your story needs to be shared. Don't be scared to seek out and discover the support that resonates with you.

Navigating the turbulent seas of sorrow is simpler when you don't have to do it alone. Remember, numerous others are suffering similar waves, and together, you may find consolation, strength, and the courage to recover. Let your voice be heard, reach out for the assistance you need, and know that you are not alone on this road.

2. Replenishing Your Cup: Self-Care is Not Selfish, It's Essential

Take care of yourself:
Grief may leave you feeling exhausted, like an empty cup giving nothing but echoes of loss. But remember, taking care of oneself isn't a luxury, it's a need. Just as you wouldn't expect a cracked cup to contain water, ignoring your own well-being hampers your potential to recover and grow.

Think of self-care as filling your cup, restoring your power and soul. Here are various ways to do so:

Listen to your body's requirements. Are you exhausted? Take a snooze. Feeling restless? Move your body via workout or dancing. Craving fresh air? Go for a walk in nature. Prioritize sleep, wholesome food, and activities that nurture your physical well-being.

Nurture your emotions. Don't repress your sentiments. Journal about them, express them via art or music, or chat to a trusted friend. Engage in things that provide you peace, such as listening to relaxing music, spending time with pets, or visiting favorite places.

Connect with your loved one's memories. Keep their spirit alive by celebrating their life in ways that are significant to you. Look at images, exchange memories, make a monument, or conduct things you loved together. This doesn't reduce your loss; it's an opportunity to commemorate their existence in your life.

Engage in activities you enjoy. Remember the things that provided you joy before the loss? Reconnect with hobbies, rekindle old passions, or try something new. Even modest moments of pleasure might add to your overall well-being.Seek professional help if required. Sometimes, self-care isn't enough. Don't hesitate to seek professional help from therapists or counselors who can give direction and support in navigating your grief journey.

Remember:
Self-care isn't selfish, it's sustainable. Taking care of yourself helps you to better care for others, including respecting the memory of your loved one.

Small steps add up. You don't need to embark on huge acts of self-care. Even five minutes of focused breathing or reading a few pages of a good book may make a difference.

Be patient and nice to yourself. Healing takes
time, and there will be good days and bad days.
Don't be disheartened by setbacks; appreciate
your accomplishments, large or small.

By filling your cup, you provide yourself with the
courage and resilience required to navigate the
waves of loss. Prioritize self-care, locate what fills
your spirit, and remember, you are deserving of
love, care, and healing.

Celebrate their life:
Keeping Their Light Alive: Celebrating the Life
You Shared

Grief creates a long shadow, yet amid its gloom,
the lively memory of your loved one still shines.
Honoring their life isn't a method to avoid pain,
but to celebrate the joy they provided to the
world, keeping their spark alive within you and
beyond.

Find methods to celebrate that feel real to you
and your loved one:

Share their stories: Gather with friends and
family and reminisce about their idiosyncrasies,
experiences, and amusing moments. Laughter

may be a great healer, reminding you of the joy
they gave to your life.

Create a memory box: Collect photographs,
letters, souvenirs, or anything that inspires joyful
memories. Looking through this treasure trove
might bring back a surge of warmth and
connection.

Visit treasured places: Did they have a favorite
park, café, or museum? Revisit these locales and
take in the memories they carry. You could even
develop a new tradition, connecting with their
spirit at these particular spots.

Embrace their passions: Did they adore music?
Play their favorite tracks and dance like nobody's
looking. Were they enthusiastic gardeners? Plant
a memorial garden in their honor. Keeping their
hobbies alive keeps their soul fresh.

Volunteer for a cause they loved about: Give
back to the community in their honor, turning
your sadness into a good activity that embodies
their beliefs.

Create something beautiful: Write a poem, create
a picture, or compose a song inspired by their

memories. Expressing your feelings via art may
be a therapeutic and healing experience.

Do not forget:
There's no right or wrong way to rejoice. Find
techniques that resonate with you, expressing
your particular bond with your loved one.

Don't let grief define your decisions. While
honoring their memories, don't forget to
appreciate life itself. Embrace pleasure, laughter,
and new experiences, knowing that they wouldn't
want you to be dominated by melancholy.

Keep their legacy alive. Share their tales with
future generations, ensuring their memory
continues to inspire and affect lives.

Celebrating your loved one's life doesn't
invalidate sadness; it weaves it into a tapestry of
love, remembrance, and eternal connection.
Embrace this chance to keep their light glowing
brightly, recognizing their presence and finding
solace in the memories you share.

Finding Strength in Connection: You Are Not Alone

Embrace support:
Grief's journey might feel like climbing a lonely mountain trail, shrouded in mist and uncertainty. But remember, the heights are designed to be attained together, not in solitude. Embracing help from others isn't a sign of weakness, but a monument to your courage and intelligence in pursuing recovery.

Reach out to your anchors of strength:
Trusted friends and family: Share your stories, your sorrows, and your hopes. Find peace in their listening ears, warm embraces, and understanding hearts. Don't shy away from asking for particular aid, whether it's a shoulder to weep on, assistance with errands, or simply someone to sit in quiet with you.

Support groups: Connect with people who understand your grief. Sharing experiences, validating feelings, and finding consolation in others' journeys may build a profound sense of connection and belonging. Online or in-person, support groups offer a secure environment for empathy and understanding.

Therapists and counselors: Trained experts give a discreet space to express your feelings without judgment and offer help for managing your sorrow. They can equip you with appropriate coping techniques and help you manage difficult feelings.

Remember:
Talking is therapeutic. Bottling up emotions may be hazardous. Finding someone you trust to listen, whether it's a loved one, therapist, or support group member, may give enormous comfort and insight.

Support comes in various kinds. It doesn't have to be long, drawn-out chats. Sharing a joke with a buddy, attending a grief-focused event, or simply having someone check in on you may all be forms of helpful connection.

You deserve to be heard. Your voice counts, your story needs to be shared. Don't be scared to seek out and discover the support that resonates with you.

Navigating the turbulent seas of sorrow is simpler when you don't have to do it alone. Remember, numerous others are suffering similar waves, and together, you may find consolation, strength, and the courage to recover. Let your voice be heard, reach out for the assistance you need, and know that you are not alone on this road.

3. Riding the Waves: Practical Tips for Difficult Days

Grief can ebb and flow, with peaceful times disrupted by crashing floods of emotion. When those intense sensations arrive, remember, you have tools in your toolbox to handle the storm. Here are some practical ideas for bad days:

Calming Your Breath:

Deep Breathing: Find a peaceful area, close your eyes, and take slow, deep breaths in your nose, holding for a few seconds, then releasing gently through your mouth. Repeat for several minutes, focusing on the rise and fall of your chest and belly.

Box Breathing: Imagine drawing a square with your breath. Inhale for a count of 4, hold for 4, exhale for 4, hold for 4, and repeat. This regulated breathing pattern helps manage your neural system.

Grounding Techniques:

5-4-3-2-1 Senses: Focus on your surroundings. Name five things you can see, four things you can touch, three things you can hear, two things you can smell, and one item you can taste. Engaging your senses helps anchor you in the present moment.

Progressive Muscle Relaxation: Tense and release distinct muscle groups in your body, one at a time, starting with your toes and working your way up. This can assist alleviate bodily tension and encourage relaxation.

Mindfulness Practices:

Guided Meditations: Many free applications and internet sites provide guided meditations particularly suited for mourning. Find one that resonates with you and follow the directions to quiet your thoughts and focus on the present moment.

Body Scans: Lie down comfortably and focus your attention on different regions of your body, recognizing any feelings without judgment. This might help you become more aware of your bodily and mental condition.

Additional Tips:

Reach out for support: Don't hesitate to phone a trustworthy friend, family member, or therapist when you're feeling overwhelmed. Talking about your feelings may be immensely useful.

Engage in activities you enjoy: Even tiny things like listening to music, reading a book, or spending time in nature may enhance your mood and bring a sense of comfort.

Be patient with yourself: Healing takes time and there will be good and terrible days. Celebrate your accomplishments, no matter how modest, and don't be disheartened by setbacks.

Remember: You are not alone on this path. These resources are intended to assist you manage the hardest days, but don't hesitate to seek professional help if required. With self-compassion, mindfulness, and the help of others, you can weather the storms and find serenity on your journey to healing.

Additional Notes:
Tailor the specific tactics to the age range of your readers. For example, younger children could

benefit from basic breathing exercises or visualizations, while older adolescents and adults might choose more complex mindfulness activities.

Consider offering links or sites where readers may discover guided meditations, relaxation exercises, and support groups.

Encourage readers to explore and find the tools that work best for them.

By giving practical ideas and encouraging readers to seek help, you may inspire them to tackle their challenging days with courage and perseverance.

4. Navigating Triggers: Anticipate and Manage the Storms Within

Grief's journey is rarely predictable. Certain events, places, even songs can operate as unanticipated triggers, triggering a surge of powerful emotions. But remember, recognizing your triggers helps you to prepare and create coping methods, navigating these storms with greater resilience.

Identifying Your Triggers:

Reflect: Think about prior circumstances, places, or experiences that have evoked powerful emotions. It may be anniversaries, special songs, certain fragrances, or simply seeing a particular object.

Journal: Keep a record of your triggers, noting the emotions they produce. This self-awareness might help you anticipate and prepare.

Seek Insights: Talk to friends, relatives, or therapists about potential triggers they've witnessed. Different views can bring significant insights.

Developing Coping Mechanisms:

Planning Makes Perfect: If you know you'll be confronting a trigger, develop tactics beforehand. Talk to a trusted friend about it, have a self-care plan in place (relaxation methods, meditation), or carry a comfortable object.

Mindful Avoidance: When feasible, carefully avoid recognized triggers, especially when you're feeling emotionally sensitive. This isn't avoidance forever, but a purposeful strategy to gain power.

Distraction is Your Ally: When a trigger suddenly hits, employ healthy distractions. Call a friend, listen to uplifting music, participate in deep breathing exercises, or focus on relaxing hobbies like coloring or gardening.

Seek Support: Don't hesitate to call on trustworthy loved ones or experts at triggering occasions. Talking things out, sharing your thoughts, and having support may be enormously beneficial.

Remember:
Triggers are usual. Everyone has them, and they don't define you or your healing process.

Preparation is crucial. By anticipating and prepping for triggers, you gain control and traverse them with more strength.

Be gentle to yourself. There will be moments when triggers catch you off guard. Forgive yourself, work on calming down, and ask out for assistance if required.

Triggers aren't obstacles, but bumps on the way to healing. By identifying them, creating coping skills, and seeking help, you may manage these obstacles with resilience and go ahead on your path with renewed strength.

Finding Sunshine in Memories: Recalling Joy despite Grief

Remember the happy times:
Grief feels heavy, like a persistent deluge. But remember, underneath the storm clouds, the sun still shines. Holding onto the pleasant memories of your loved one isn't a betrayal of your grief, but a valuable tool for healing.

Imagine uncovering a treasure trove packed with happy memories:

Laughter-filled memories: Recall shared jokes, hilarious anecdotes, or playful times that made you both scream in laughter. Let their happy echoes lighten your heart.

Adventures and milestones: Relive beloved moments, big or little, from exploring new locations to celebrating victories. Remember the shared grins and the excitement in their eyes.

Gestures of love and kindness: Rekindle memories of simple gestures of affection, a warm hug, a thoughtful gift, or just their kind words. Let their compassion melt your spirit.

Unique quirks and passions: Reflect on their personality, their interests, the things that made them genuinely unique. Find consolation in recalling who they were and what brought them delight.

Weaving these memories into your life can be very healing:

Share tales with others: Keep their memory alive by sharing amusing anecdotes, meaningful experiences, or inspiring stories with loved ones. Laughter and shared memories may be immensely therapeutic.

Create concrete reminders: Make a scrapbook packed with images, souvenirs, or quotations that recall positive memories. Surround yourself with these reminders of their love and brightness.

Visit beloved locations: Revisit areas you shared, whether it's a favorite park, restaurant, or vacation destination. Immerse yourself in the memories and feel their presence near you.

Engage in things they loved: Did they like painting? Pick up a brush! Did they appreciate nature walks? Lace up your shoes and explore! Reconnecting with their passions keeps their soul alive.

Remember:
Healing isn't about forgetting. It's about learning to carry your loved one's memory with love and joy, alongside your pain.

Not all memories are sunshine and rainbows. Sometimes, tough experiences can also include great lessons and insights. Honor all parts of your common past.

Be kind with yourself. Don't force joy if it doesn't come naturally. Allow yourself to feel all your emotions, but open your heart to the warmth of beloved memories when you're ready.

Remembering the wonderful moments isn't a rejection of your sadness, but a celebration of the love you shared. Let the sunlight of good memories peak through the clouds, guiding you towards healing and reminding you that your loved one's pleasure lives on within you.

Remember, You're on the Right Path: Kindness is
Your Guiding Light

Be gentle to yourself:
Grief is a marathon, not a sprint. It's a twisting
route with valleys of sadness and sun-drenched
summits of recall. On this trip, remember:
kindness to oneself is not a luxury, it's the
gasoline that drives you ahead.

Be patient with your progress:

Healing isn't linear. There will be good days and
terrible days, tears and joy, failures and
breakthroughs. Celebrate every step, no matter
how tiny.

Don't compare your trip to others'. We all mourn
individually, at our own time. Focus on your own
healing process and trust your intuition.

Forgive yourself for feeling depressed. Sadness,
wrath, perplexity - all these feelings are valid.
Acknowledge them, express them properly, and
then let them go.

Celebrate even the seemingly modest victories:

Getting out of bed and tackling the day is a success. Taking a shower is a win. Talking to a buddy is a victory. Each step, great or small, matters.

Be proud of your resilience. Facing grief needs enormous strength. Acknowledge your courage and potential to heal.

Find delight in the simple things. A magnificent sunset, a shared joke, a nice gesture - these moments of brightness may fuel your spirit even during loss.

Treat yourself with the same kindness you would offer a loved one:

Listen to your requirements. Are you exhausted? Rest. Feeling overwhelmed? Take a rest. Prioritize activities that offer you comfort and foster your well-being.

Surround yourself with supportive individuals. Seek out friends, relatives, or therapists who give understanding and encouragement. Don't be frightened to depend on their strength.

Engage in self-care habits that nurture your spirit. Whether it's reading, meditating, spending time in nature, or simply taking a deep breath, identify what feeds your spirit.

Remember:
You are not alone. Countless people have walked this journey before you, and many are traveling it with you. Seek help and connect with those who understand.

Grief doesn't define you. It's a part of your narrative, but it doesn't remove your strength, resilience, or the joy that still lives inside you.

You are strong, capable, and worthy of love and happiness. Believe in yourself and in your abilities to heal.

As you traverse this road, remember to be your own best cheerleader. Offer yourself kindness, patience, and understanding. With each stride forward, you're coming closer to a place of serenity and healing. Keep going, one pleasant moment at a time.

Healing is a personal journey, and you will go forward at your own rate. Remember, you are strong, resilient, and cherished. This chapter is

your companion, bringing comfort and direction
as you traverse the route ahead.

Chapter 9:

Sharing the Journey of Grief with Children, Teens, & Young Adults: Hope and New Beginnings

The pain of loss is universal, although it appears differently across age groups. This chapter discusses the delicate work of leading children, teenagers, and young adults through the maze of loss towards the bright road of hope and renewed joy.

1. Children:

You're completely right! Those are two key elements for assisting children through bereavement. To dive deeper, here are some other ideas:

Language Matters:
Tailor the explanation to their age and understanding: For younger children, emphasis on specific concepts such as saying "Grandma can't come play anymore because her body stopped working." As kids age, gradually introduce complicated phrases like "death" and "passed away," always explaining them honestly and carefully.

Use familiar analogies and comparisons: Help kids grasp death with realistic concepts like a falling leaf or a butterfly leaving its cocoon.

Be consistent: Use the same terminology again to reduce misunderstanding and bring comfort in familiar language.

Answer their inquiries honestly and directly: Even if their queries seem tough or repeated, address them with age-appropriate honesty. Avoid stating phrases like "They're in a better place" or "God needed them," since they could engender misunderstanding or anxiety.

Embrace Openness:
Create a safe area for all emotions: Let them know that there are no "bad" sentiments when it comes to grieving. Encourage them to weep, yell, draw furious images, or express themselves anyway they feel comfortable.

Validate their emotions: Don't ignore their unhappiness or attempt to cheer them up too fast. Simply recognizing their sentiments with comments like "I see you're sad" or "It's okay to feel angry" may be extremely calming.

Use alternative instruments for expression: If they struggle to communicate their feelings, give creative outlets like sketching, playing with play-dough, or constructing with blocks. These can help them handle emotions nonverbally.

Be patient: Grieving takes time, and children may regress in growth or experience setbacks. Be patient and understanding, giving ongoing support and reassurance.

Remember, even young children are capable of comprehending and processing loss in their own way. By using clear language, establishing a safe environment for emotions, and offering creative avenues for expression, you may help them traverse this challenging road and find healing.

Rituals & Routines:
Creating anchors of stability: When a loved one dies, children's world becomes uncertain. Establishing familiar routines and rituals promotes a sense of normalcy and security.

Honoring the lost loved one: Integrate traditions that commemorate the deceased's memory into daily life. These might be simple activities like saying goodnight to a photo, creating their favorite food, or reading a treasured bedtime tale.

Age-appropriate engagement: Adjust rituals based on the child's age and knowledge. Younger children may enjoy blowing bubbles for their grandfather who enjoyed the park, while older youngsters could volunteer at their grandma's favorite charity.

Memory boxes: Encourage constructing a box filled with images, items, and memorabilia reflecting the departed. Sharing these artifacts and reminiscing joyful memories may be a soothing routine.

Nature rituals: Planting a tree, releasing balloons (eco-friendly alternatives encouraged), or sprinkling birdseed might be symbolic methods to connect with the departed loved one and convey sentiments.

Letters and storytelling: Encourage youngsters to write letters to the deceased expressing their thoughts or create tales about their memories together. These may be valued treasures and therapeutic outlets.

Play and Expression:
Play therapy's power: Play helps children to process emotions nonverbally and explore themes of loss and sorrow in a secure, regulated setting.

Tailoring to age and development: Storytelling with puppets, dolls, or stuffed animals works well for younger children. Drawing, painting, or sculpting can be expressive outlets for older ones.

Music and movement: Encourage singing songs about missing someone, making dances expressing their emotions, or utilizing instruments to convey their sentiments nonverbally.

Imaginary play: Allowing youngsters to construct scenarios where they engage with the deceased in their imagination can be useful for processing sorrow and exploring emotions.

Role-playing: Role-playing circumstances like attending to the funeral or talking to friends about the loss might help them practice coping techniques and acquire confidence in expressing their thoughts.

Books and games: Utilize age-appropriate books and activities particularly developed to help youngsters understand and cope with loss. These can be excellent tools for opening talks and offering assistance.

Remember:
Involve the youngster in establishing these routines and picking activities. This empowers them and improves their participation.

Be patient and supportive. There's no right or wrong way to grieve, and each youngster will express their feelings differently.

Maintain open communication. Encourage them to talk about their feelings and answer their queries honestly.

Seek professional help if required. If you are overwhelmed or concerned about your kid's sorrow, don't hesitate to seek professional help from a therapist or counselor specialized in child bereavement.

By recognizing the importance of rituals, routines, and play, you can help children navigate the complicated feelings of sorrow and discover healthy methods to express themselves and begin to heal.

2. Teenagers:

Validate their individuality: Recognizing that each teen grieves differently is vital. Don't compare their experience to others or try to force them into a set schedule for healing. Accept their individual feelings and behaviors.

Acknowledge the complete spectrum: Teens typically battle with complicated feelings including rage, guilt, bewilderment, and solitude. Allow them to communicate their sentiments without judgment. Dismissing or dismissing their fury as "teenage angst" might push them further away.

Create a secure environment for confiding: Teens might not readily open up, but ensure you're present when they need someone to talk to. This might be through open-ended inquiries like "How are you feeling today?" or simply being there and lending a listening ear. Avoid probing or pressuring talks.

Listen actively and non-judgmentally: When they do confide, focus on active listening. This includes giving them your whole attention, eliminating distractions, and acknowledging their feelings. Use comments like "I understand this must be difficult" or "It's okay to feel angry" to demonstrate empathy and acceptance.

Respect their privacy: While being available, respect their need for space. Imposing continuous communication might feel overbearing. Let them know you're there for them, but don't urge them to chat if they're not ready.

Open the door for unpleasant conversations: Teens could have questions about death, the afterlife, or even their own mortality. Don't shy away from these interactions. Be honest and provide age-appropriate explanations, admitting the unknowns and giving your personal opinions if comfortable.

Beyond words: Actions speak louder than words. Show your support via daily gestures: making their favorite food, watching a movie together, or simply sitting in comfortable quiet. Sometimes, being present without words may be the most potent kind of support.

Remember:
Teenagers often communicate sadness through indirect methods including mood swings, changes in behavior, or seclusion. Be patient and watchful.

Encourage them to connect with trusted friends or mentors who could understand their situation better. Peer support may be crucial.

Be attentive of your own feelings. Processing your own loss is necessary, but avoid burdening your teen with your troubles.

Seek professional help if required. If you're concerned about your teen's mental health or they're showing self-harm habits, reaching out to a therapist or counselor can give professional help.

By understanding the complexity of their feelings, establishing a safe space for conversation, and offering steadfast support, you may help kids navigate the rough waters of sorrow and discover their own road to healing.

The power of peer support:
Connecting with shared experiences: Joining support groups designed for grieving teenagers

gives a secure area where they may connect with others who understand their sorrow and feelings. Sharing stories and sharing mutual support can be immensely affirming and therapeutic.

Breaking down isolation: Grief might feel isolated, but interacting with friends who've endured similar losses can overcome that sensation. They can connect to one another's problems and give empathy and companionship.

Learning from shared coping mechanisms: Support groups and peer relationships help teenagers to exchange coping techniques and explore new ways to manage their loss. This can empower them and give vital strategies for controlling their emotions.

Facilitating connections: Encourage your teen to investigate internet forums, local support groups, or grief therapy seminars particularly created for teens. You may assist them explore possibilities and perhaps accompany them initially if required.

Finding meaning and purpose:
Channeling emotions into action: Volunteering for causes linked to their loss, joining community initiatives, or helping those in need can offer a

sense of purpose and channel their sadness into good action.

Returning to passions: Encourage them to re-engage with hobbies or activities they liked before the loss. Immersing oneself in something they're enthusiastic about might bring consolation and distract them from unwanted feelings.

Exploring new avenues: If prior interests no longer retain appeal, encourage them to pursue new ones. Taking an art class, learning a new instrument, or joining a sports team may give new experiences, increase confidence, and stimulate personal growth.

Creating and expressing: Encourage creative expression via writing, music, photography, or any other media that connects with them. This may be a powerful approach to process emotions, examine their sorrow, and find new ways to interpret their experiences.

Finding beauty in ordinary moments: Guide children to enjoy the minor delights in life, like spending time in nature, listening to music, or seeing a beautiful sunset. Focusing on these pleasant experiences may be a source of strength and remind them that beauty still exists.

Remember:
Finding meaningful hobbies requires time and exploration. Encourage your teen to explore and see what connects with them.

Focus on progress, not perfection. There will be ups and downs. Celebrate little accomplishments and provide ongoing encouragement even when they struggle to engage in activities.

Respect their decisions. Don't press children into activities they're not ready for. Allow them to explore and find their own route to recovery.

Seek professional help if required. If your teen struggles to cope or participates in dangerous activities, don't hesitate to seek professional treatment from a therapist or counselor specialized in teenage grieving.

By establishing peer relationships, promoting meaningful activities, and showing unshakable support, you may help your adolescent find consolation, purpose, and finally discover a route ahead that allows them to live a fulfilled life, even in the face of sadness.

3. Young Adults: Respecting individuality:

Young adults are creating their own identities and freedom. Recognize their particular requirements and preferences while delivering help. Avoid pushing your own agenda or ideas of how they "should" mourn.

Tailored support: Engage in open talks to discover their preferred techniques of dealing with loss. Some might desire open conversation, while others would prefer silent support and distance. Respect their boundaries and change your approach accordingly.

Provide resources, not mandates: Instead of prescribing their route, provide a choice of resources like support groups, therapeutic alternatives, or books on bereavement. Allow them to choose what resonates with them and promotes their particular healing path.

Navigating existential complexities:
Brace for hard conversations: Young adults typically wrestle with serious concerns about life, death, and their own mortality in the wake of loss. Be prepared to engage in these talks with honesty and kindness.

Acknowledge the unknown: Don't shy away from acknowledging that you don't have all the answers. It's appropriate to acknowledge the intricacies and mysteries of life and loss alongside them.

Validate their fears: It's reasonable to anticipate future loss after experiencing considerable grief. Validate their fears and give help in exploring coping techniques like mindfulness practices or journaling.

Urge healthy exploration: While respecting their limits, gently urge them to engage in open-ended talks about life's purpose, finding meaning, and negotiating their unique beliefs in the midst of loss.

Remember:
Balance support with independence: Offer constant assistance without encroaching on their space or decision-making. Let them know you're there, but trust them to handle their loss in their own manner.

Respect their demand for privacy: Some young adults might choose to manage their feelings inside. Respect their desire for space and avoid pressuring them to chat if they're not ready.

Be conscious of your own emotions: It's vital to grieve your own loss, but avoid burdening them with your troubles. Seek help from other adults or professionals if required.

Professional help is valid: Don't hesitate to promote professional treatment if they look overwhelmed, struggle to function everyday, or engage in unhealthy coping techniques. Therapists specialized in young adult bereavement can give vital information and support.

By acknowledging their individuality, creating space for hard talks, and providing steadfast support without judgment, you may become a light of compassion and strength for young adults traveling the challenging journey of grieving. Remember, every journey is unique, and your responsibility is to walk alongside them, not prescribe their course.

Exploring Healthy Coping Mechanisms:

Empowering Self-Care: Encourage young individuals to emphasize self-care habits that promote their physical and emotional wellness. Exercise, proper food, and enough sleep build the framework for emotional resiliency.

Mindfulness and Relaxation Techniques: Introduce them to techniques like meditation, yoga, or deep breathing exercises. These can help manage stress, anxiety, and intrusive thoughts connected to mourning.

Creative Expression: Provide opportunities for creative expression like painting, writing, music, or dancing. These can bring emotional relief, process loss in a non-verbal way, and perhaps lead to unexpected discoveries about themselves.

Finding Meaning and Purpose:

Volunteerism and Community Engagement: Encourage them to connect with topics they care about through volunteering or community initiatives. Helping others may create a sense of purpose and promote connection, fighting feelings of loneliness.

Personal Passions and ambitions: Support their pursuit of hobbies, interests, or academic ambitions. Immersing oneself in things they like may provide joy, boost confidence, and create a feeling of success despite loss.

Personal Growth and Exploration: Encourage them to explore new hobbies, attend lessons, or embark on personal growth adventures. This can give distractions, stimulate new hobbies, and help individuals rethink their life post-loss.

Reconstructing Identity: Recognize that loss might influence their sense of self. Support them in examining their shifting identity, beliefs, and ambitions in the context of their loss.

Seeking Professional Help:

Recognizing Deeper Struggles: Be cautious of indicators of crippling anxiety, despair, or difficulties functioning in everyday life, such as missing duties, retreating from social engagement, or participating in dangerous activities.

Destigmatizing Therapy: Normalize obtaining professional treatment as a form of self-care and proactive support. Discuss therapists specialized in young adult bereavement and urge them to investigate this option without judgment.

Offering Ongoing Support: Let them know you're there for them even if they select professional aid. Remind them that seeking help is a show of

courage and may provide them with vital tools
for navigating their individual grieving journey.

Remember:
Healing is not linear: There will be good days and
terrible days. Encourage them to be patient with
themselves and appreciate minor
accomplishments along the road.

Their route is unique: Don't compare their
healing process to others. Offer help according to
their requirements and respect their particular
decisions.

Empathy and understanding: Listen intently and
affirm their emotions without judgment. Offer a
secure area where people may disclose their
concerns, doubts, and hopes.

Celebrate their resilience: Acknowledge their
strength and courage in handling loss. Remind
them that even despite sadness, they have the
capacity to mold their destiny and find purpose in
their lives.

By giving direction, supporting investigation, and
encouraging professional treatment when
required, you may encourage young adults to
negotiate the intricacies of sorrow, develop

healthy coping methods, and eventually find their own road to recovery and a meaningful future.

4. Hope and New Beginnings: Nurturing Joy in the Shadow of Loss

It's vital to underline that finding joy again isn't about ignoring the lost loved one. It's about honoring their memories while creating space for new experiences and enjoyment.

While loss creates a lengthy shadow, hope, like a tenacious vine, makes its way through, seeking brightness and resilience. In this chapter, we examine developing optimism and discovering fresh beginnings, even despite the agony of loss.

Focus on Positive Memories:
Cultivate a space for happy remembrance: Encourage children, teenagers, and young adults to share loving recollections of the lost loved one. Create memory boxes, scrapbooks, or digital memorials packed with images, stories, and things that trigger pleasant feelings.

Celebrate their impact: Reflect on how the departed enhanced their life and the world around them. This encourages thankfulness and keeps their memory alive in a pleasant light.

Encourage sending letters expressing thanks, planting trees in their honor, or participating in activities they liked.

Humor as a therapeutic balm: Share amusing tales, inside jokes, or lighter moments that bring laughter and warmth to their recollection. Humor can be a great tool for reducing the load of loss and reminding them of the joy their loved one offered.

Celebrate Milestones:
Big and little victories: Acknowledge and appreciate personal achievements, both great and little, when they occur. Graduations, birthdays, new successes, or even commonplace victories like learning a new skill or conquering a personal problem. Celebrate these marks of life's continued journey, honoring the memory of the lost one by continuing to live and develop.

Customs with a twist: Reimagine beloved customs shared with the departed. Bake their favorite cookies together, visit their favorite park, or watch their favorite movie, adding new components that represent personal growth and appreciate their continuous presence in your life.

New traditions for new chapters: Encourage the formation of new customs that honor the lost loved one while looking forward to the future. Plant a tree together on their birthday, volunteer for a cause they liked, or launch a scholarship in their name. These create hope by respecting their legacy and crafting a future they would be proud of.

Remember:
Hope is a journey, not a destination: Emphasize that rediscovering joy again doesn't imply forgetting the lost one. It's about learning to carry their memory with love and appreciation while embracing the possibility of new experiences and pleasure.

Respect unique processes: Grief manifests differently for everyone. Encourage each individual to develop their own unique methods to celebrate life and foster hope, giving support and understanding along their path.

Offer expert guidance: If grieving becomes overpowering or impairs everyday living, suggest getting professional treatment from therapists or counselors specialized in grief and loss. They can give vital tools and help for navigating this challenging route.

By recalling the joy, celebrating milestones, and promoting hope, we may assist children, teenagers, and young adults go beyond the darkness of loss and find the fortitude to embrace new beginnings, taking the love and memories of their loved ones with them in their hearts.

Finding New Passions and Goals:
Exploration and Experimentation: Encourage young individuals to explore new interests, passions, and ambitions without judgment. This may be anything from taking a pottery class to volunteering at an animal shelter, learning a new language, or beginning a personal project. Experimentation helps people to uncover latent abilities, connect with new communities, and find purpose outside of their loss.

Honoring the Lost While Looking Forward: As they explore new areas, help them to think on how their loved one would have supported or inspired their activities. This helps individuals connect their present to their past and carry their loved one's memories with them in a meaningful way.

Celebrating modest Victories: Acknowledge and appreciate even modest steps ahead in their path. Mastering a new ability, conquering a hurdle, or just finding delight in a new pastime - these milestones are building blocks for a brighter future.

Hope is a Journey, Not a Destination:
Navigating Good and Bad Days: Reinforce that the journey towards hope is rarely straightforward. There will be wonderful days filled with sunshine and dismal days covered in storm clouds. Remind them that sorrow is a natural process, and these changes are typical.

Practicing Self-Compassion: Encourage them to be patient and compassionate with themselves during this process. Celebrate their fortitude in facing loss, accept their shortcomings without judgment, and provide unflinching support throughout.

Celebrating Every Step Forward: Focus on progress, not perfection. Every step forward, every difficulty overcome, every moment of delight discovered is a success. Encourage children to celebrate these steps, no matter how tiny, as they pave the path for a brighter future.

Remember:
Uniqueness in Healing: Each young adult's healing journey will be unique. Respect their particular pace, interests, and coping techniques. Offer individualized assistance that encourages people to develop their own path to purpose and hope.

The Power of Community: Encourage them to connect with friends, family, support groups, or online communities where they may share experiences, receive encouragement, and feel understood. Community gives a sense of belonging and promotes the message that they are not alone.

Professional aid is a Strength: Don't hesitate to promote professional aid if they suffer trouble coping, struggle with everyday functioning, or feel overwhelmed by their emotions. Therapists specialized in mourning can give significant skills and assistance in navigating this tough route.

By encouraging the confidence to explore, recognizing their growth, and reminding them of the underlying power inside, you may help young adults discover new purpose in their life, even amidst the shadow of loss. Let them know that hope is a journey, not a destination, and that every step forward, no matter how tiny, is a stride towards a brighter future filled with significance and joy.

Remember, every individual grieves differently. By personalizing your approach, giving constant support, and validating their emotions, you may assist children, teenagers, and young adults traverse the journey of sorrow and discover the promise for fresh beginnings that lies ahead.

Chapter 10:

You Are Not Alone: Finding Hope and Solidarity on Your Grief Journey

Loss is a common feeling, yet the road through mourning may feel solitary and lonely. This chapter seeks to remind you, dear reader, that you are not alone. Many people walk beside you, experiencing similar difficulties and knowing the depths of your feelings. Whether you're a kid, adolescent, or young adult, know that support and tools exist to assist you walk your own road towards recovery.

1. Understanding Your Grief

Grief is a complicated and personal feeling. It is not restricted to melancholy, but involves a wide variety of emotions: wrath, bewilderment, fear, guilt, disbelief, loneliness, and even joy via cherished memories. These sensations are all real and natural, and they may ebb and flow in unforeseen ways.

Always remember that there is no "right" or "wrong" way to grieve. Your path is unique to you, molded by your relationship with the departed loved one, your personality, and life events. Embrace your feelings, allow yourself to feel them fully, and realize that it's good not to have all the solutions.

Grief is undoubtedly a difficult and personal journey, and to properly comprehend your own experience, it's necessary to go deeper into the emotional environment you're traversing. Here's a more complete look at the numerous components of grief:

Emotions in the Kaleidoscope:

Sadness: This is the most usually connected emotion with sadness, a genuine sorrow for the loss. It might emerge as tears, emptiness, a lack of drive, or a craving for the person or circumstance that's gone.

Anger: This can seem paradoxical, but anger can be a natural response to feeling helpless and mistreated. It might be aimed at yourself, the person who died, or even events beyond your control.

Confusion: The world feels upside down following a loss, and it's reasonable to feel confused about what's happening to you and how to move ahead.

Fear: This feeling might arise from the uncertainty of the future, the fear of more losses, or even the fear of your own emotions.

Guilt: You could doubt your behavior or comments before the loss, leading to emotions of guilt and self-blame. Remember, these are typical emotions, and guilt doesn't define you.

Skepticism: Especially with rapid losses, your mind could struggle to grasp the reality of the event, resulting in a sensation of skepticism.

Loneliness: The absence of your loved one can leave a large hole, leading to feelings of isolation and loneliness.

Joy via memories: Grief is not simply about grief. Remembering cherished times with your loved one can provide flashes of joy and comfort, reminding you of the love and connection you shared.

Understanding the Waves:
These feelings don't arrive in a regular order or stay steady. They may ebb and flow in unpredictable waves, leaving you feeling overwhelmed at times and oddly numb at others. This is absolutely normal. Be kind with yourself and allow yourself to feel these emotions fully without judgment.

Individuality is Key:
Remember, everyone's mourning path is unique. It's shaped by numerous factors:

Your relationship with the deceased: The closeness and type of your relationship will considerably affect your mourning experience.

Your personality: Some persons are inherently more outspoken of their emotions, while others tend to internalize them.

Your life experiences: Past losses, coping methods, and cultural standards can all impact how you mourn.

Embracing the Journey:
Instead of striving to control or conceal your emotions, try to accept them as part of your healing process. Acknowledge them, affirm them,

and allow yourself to experience them fully. Remember, it's acceptable not to have all the answers. This is a voyage of self-discovery and acceptance.

Additional Points:
It's vital to discern between healthy mourning and difficult sorrow. While sadness and other feelings are anticipated, if your grieving becomes debilitating and interferes with your everyday life for an extended period, finding expert support is vital.

Talking about your feelings with trustworthy friends, family, or a therapist may be immensely useful in processing your emotions and receiving support.

Remember, you are not alone on this path. Many tools and support groups are available to assist you negotiate your sorrow.

Note:
Understanding your emotions and their complexities is vital to navigating your particular mourning journey. Be gentle with yourself, seek assistance when required, and realize that recovery is possible, even if the route appears long and tough.

2. Finding Solidarity and Support

While sorrow might feel lonely, know that you are not alone. Here are several methods to find unity and support:

Talking to Family and Friends:
Grief may be an isolated experience, but speaking out to loved ones can be immensely beneficial in navigating this tough road. Here's a deeper explanation of why and how chatting to family and friends may generate a sense of connectedness and give important support:

Benefits of Sharing Your Feelings:
Validation and Understanding: Sharing your emotions helps people to acknowledge the reality of your feelings and give understanding, which can be immensely reassuring. Hearing "I understand how you feel" may go a long way in minimizing loneliness and validating your experience.

Reduced Shame and Guilt: Grief frequently brings layers of shame and guilt. By sharing your concerns freely, you allow others to give comfort and perspective, thereby relieving these responsibilities.

Connection and Belonging: Sharing your story builds a stronger connection with your loved ones. You'll learn how people are coping with the loss, generating a feeling of shared experience and belonging.

Emotional Release: Talking may work as a cathartic release, helping you to process your feelings in a healthy way and perhaps lower their severity.

Practical help: Sharing your requirements with loved ones might open doors to practical help. They could give help with errands, childcare, or simply a listening ear when you need it most.

Tips for Effective Communication:
Start Small: Don't feel forced to disclose everything at once. Begin with baby steps, discussing what seems comfortable and progressively opening up as you feel safe.

Find the Right Listener: Choose persons who are good listeners, compassionate, and non-judgmental. Look for folks who have suffered loss themselves or are comfortable with emotional talks.

Create Boundaries: It's appropriate to create boundaries around what you're comfortable sharing and how much help you need. Don't feel pressured to overshare if it feels overwhelming.

Be Direct: Sometimes, simply addressing your requirements helps loved ones understand how they can best support you. Whether it's wanting a shoulder to weep on, help with a certain chore, or simply someone to listen without judgment, be explicit about what would be helpful.

Practice Active Listening: Pay attention to how your loved ones respond and acknowledge their feelings as well. This two-way communication creates deeper connection and enhances your support system.

Remember:
Not everyone will be a good listener: It's acceptable if someone doesn't answer as you hoped. Focus on connecting with those who give true support and understanding.

There's no "right" way to talk about grief: Share your feelings truthfully, in whichever way seems most comfortable for you.

Talking doesn't decrease your grief: It's a tool to help you process your feelings and connect with others, not a miraculous remedy to eliminate your misery.

By opening up to trustworthy friends and family, you may develop a powerful support system that eases the burden of loss and helps you navigate your recovery journey. Remember, you are not alone, and seeking out for connection is a sign of strength, not weakness.

Connecting with Support Groups: Finding Strength in Shared Understanding

Grief might feel isolated, but joining a support group can be a strong remedy. Here's a deeper look into why and how connecting with others who understand your loss can be very affirming and comforting:

Benefits of Joining a Support Group:

Shared Understanding: You'll be surrounded by folks who have endured similar losses, generating an immediate sense of belonging and understanding. Sharing your experience without attempting to explain the subtleties of grieving may be immensely freeing.

Validation of Emotions: Grieving encompasses a spectrum of emotions, and support groups give a safe venue to express them all without judgment. You'll discover people who understand your rage, despair, uncertainty, and even moments of delight amidst the suffering.

Learning from Others: Hearing how others cope with their sorrow can give significant insights and solutions that you can apply to your own journey. You could discover new coping techniques, tools, or viewpoints that can be immensely beneficial.

Reduced Isolation: Sharing your experiences and connecting with those who "get it" may dramatically lessen feelings of isolation and loneliness. You'll discover you're not alone in your loss, and this may be immensely consoling.

Hope and Inspiration: Witnessing others navigate their grieving journey and discover resilience can bring hope and inspiration for your own road. Seeing others recover might motivate you to believe in your own healing ability.

Finding the Right Support Group:
Specificity: Consider joining a group specialized to your unique loss (e.g., loss of a spouse, kid, parent, pet) or loss type (e.g., suicide, unexpected death). This enables for greater connection and shared experiences.

Format: Choose a format that matches your needs. In-person groups allow face-to-face connection, while online groups give flexibility and anonymity. Consider your comfort level and preferences.

Location and Accessibility: Find a group that's convenient for you to attend, whether it's in your local neighborhood or online. Consider concerns like transportation, daycare, and technology availability.

Facilitation: Some groups are facilitated by experts, while others are peer-led. Explore possibilities and pick a place where you feel comfortable sharing and interacting.

Tips for Making the Most of Support Groups:
Be Open and Honest: Share your experiences truthfully within your comfort zone. Vulnerability may enhance ties and create trust.

Actively Listen: Pay attention to others' stories and provide assistance when appropriate. Building a supportive community goes both ways.

Respect Boundaries: Be cognizant of individual experiences and avoid comparing your trip to others. Focus on your own healing and progress.

Take Breaks: Don't feel pressured to attend every meeting or provide every information. Prioritize your well-being and take breaks when required.

Seek Additional Support: Support groups are a useful resource, but they might not meet all your requirements. Consider individual treatment or other sources of assistance alongside the group.

Remember:
Not every group is a perfect fit: Don't hesitate to try multiple groups until you find one that feels comfortable and helpful.

It takes time to create trust: Be patient and give yourself time to connect with others. The benefits of support groups generally develop gradually.

Focus on your journey: While learning from others is essential, realize that your sorrow is unique. Use the group as a tool to help your personal recovery journey.

By joining with a support group, you can find a great source of strength, understanding, and hope during your grieving journey. Remember, you are not alone, and seeking out for assistance is a bold step towards recovery.

Seek professional help: If you find yourself struggling to manage, reaching out to a therapist or counselor can give essential direction and support.

Here are some sites to help you locate support:

The Dougy Center: [https://www.dougy.org/]

The National Center for Grieving Children and Families: [https://www.childrengrieve.org/]

The Jed Foundation:
[https://www.jedfoundation.org/]

The National Alliance for Grieving Children & Families

The Trevor Project:
[https://www.thetrevorproject.org/] (For
LGBTQ+ adolescents)

For children:

Sesame Street in Communities: Helping Children
with Grief:

The Compassionate Friends:
[https://www.compassionatefriends.org/]

Remember: Seeking help is a show of strength,
not weakness. Don't hesitate to seek out and
connect with those who can give support and
understanding on your path.

3. Finding Hope Amidst Grief

While the agony of loss may feel overwhelming,
know that recovery is attainable. Even at the
worst moments, there is hope. Here are some
strategies to find hope on your mourning
journey:

Finding Hope Amidst Grief: Rekindling the Light of Positive Memories

While grieving brings waves of sadness, it's crucial to realize that hope may still exist among the agony. Focusing on the happy recollections of your loved one may be a tremendous source of comfort and inspiration as you walk your recovery path. Here are various methods to achieve this:

Celebrating Their Life:

Share stories: Gather with friends and relatives to share cherished memories and hilarious tales about your loved one. Laughter and recollection may produce a profound sense of connection and delight.

Create a memory box: Collect significant stuff like photographs, notes, trinkets, or artwork that remind you of them. Having these concrete mementos close by might bring comfort and elicit joyful memories.

Visit cherished places: If your loved one had a favorite park, restaurant, or vacation area, visit there to reminisce about shared events and connect with happy memories.

Plan a memorial ceremony or ritual: This may be a personalized way to commemorate their life and show your love and loss. It might be as simple as planting a tree in their honor or as complex as a community celebration packed with music, readings, and shared anecdotes.

Engage in things they enjoyed: Did they adore baking? Cooking their favorite food might conjure their presence and trigger good memories. Did they enjoy a certain sport? Participating in that activity might be a way to respect their memory and feel close to them.

Nurturing Your Well-being:
Embrace joy: Don't feel guilty for experiencing moments of delight or laughing. It doesn't reduce the love you had for your loved one; it's a normal aspect of life and healing.

Practice gratitude: Reflect on the positive parts of your life, the people you adore, and the nice things you still have. Gratitude may redirect your perspective and foster a sense of optimism.

Engage in self-care: Prioritize healthy food, exercise, and relaxation techniques to manage stress and preserve your mental and physical well-being. Taking care of oneself is vital for processing loss and finding strength.

Connect with nature: Spending time in nature has proven advantages for mental health. Go on walks in the park, listen to the birds chirping, or simply sit under a tree and breathe deeply. Immersing oneself in nature may provide tranquility and perspective.

Remember:
Grieving is not linear: There will be good days and awful days. Allow yourself to feel your emotions fully without judgment.

Healing takes time: Be patient with yourself and your process. Don't compare your trip to others'.

You are not alone: Seek help from family, friends, therapy, or grieving support groups. Connecting with those who understand may make a world of difference.

By cherishing the wonderful memories of your loved one, practicing self-care, and developing hope, you may find consolation and strength despite the darkness of mourning. Remember, light still exists, ready to be rekindled, and healing is attainable, one step at a time.

Rekindling Joy: Engaging in Activities You Love After Loss

Grief may leave you feeling numb and disconnected from the things that formerly provided you joy. But remember, finding joy despite the sadness is not insulting your loved one's memories. It's an essential component of your recovery process and a method to reconnect with life's beauty. Here's how partaking in things you like may provide comfort and hope:

Finding Your Spark:
Reflect on what provided you delight before: Think back to activities you actually loved, those that made you lose track of time or brought a grin to your face. This might be anything from playing music to reading, hiking to cooking, dancing to volunteering.

Start small: Don't pressure yourself to jump back into everything at once. Choose one or two hobbies you are drawn to and start with minor commitments. Even 15 minutes can make a difference.

Be adaptable and open: If an activity feels overwhelming, adjust it or try something different. Maybe reading a brief poem instead of a complete book, listening to one song instead of a whole album, or taking a short walk instead of a long excursion.

Embrace new discoveries: Loss can offer doors to new pursuits. Maybe you find a love for art, gardening, or learning a new language. Be open to exploring hobbies you haven't tried before.

The Power of Enjoyable Activities:

Connection to life: Engaging in things you like reconnects you with the vibrancy and beauty of life. It reminds you of what makes you distinct and generates a feeling of purpose.

Emotional release: It gives a healthy channel for expressing and processing your feelings. Laughter, creativity, and physical activity may be important instruments for emotional release and stress reduction.

Sense of accomplishment: Completing activities and acquiring new abilities, even modest ones, enhances your confidence and self-esteem, reminding you of your strength and potential to go forward.

Social connection: Participating in activities with others helps create social relationships and prevent feelings of loneliness. Join a group, take a lesson, or simply share your passions with pals.

Mindfulness and presence: Focusing on the present moment through joyful activities can be a sort of mindfulness, helping you separate from stress and find calm in the here and now.

Remember:
There's no right or wrong way: Do what feels good for you, regardless of what others say.

Listen to your body: If an activity feels depleting, take a break or do something alternative.

Progress over perfection: Celebrate minor successes and focus on the fun, not perfection.

Honor your loved one: You might combine hobbies you enjoyed with your loved one, or dedicate your endeavors to their memory.

By reconnecting with activities you like, you expose yourself to a road of recovery and find the joy that still lives inside you. Remember, the sun shines stronger after darkness, and your road towards recovering your happiness has already begun.

Finding Strength in Tiny Triumphs: Setting Small Goals and Celebrating Progress During Grief

Grief is a marathon, not a sprint. There will be days when every step feels heavy, and others when a spark of optimism breaks through. Setting tiny, reasonable objectives and applauding your achievement, no matter how little, may be a valuable aid for navigating this challenging trip.

Why Small Goals Make a Big Difference: Manageable and Motivating: Large, distant objectives might feel overpowering, leading to despair. Small, realistic goals seem within grasp, offering a sense of control and inspiration to keep moving ahead.

Emphasis on Progress, Not Perfection: Celebrating tiny triumphs helps change your emphasis from the immensity of the loss to the progress you're making, no matter how gradual. This encourages self-compassion and builds confidence in your abilities to recover.

Breaking Down Big Mountains: Think of a major goal as a mountain and each tiny objective as a step towards the peak. Each step mastered pushes you closer to the top, reminding you of your strength and tenacity.

Setting Meaningful Goals:
Align with Your Values: Consider what's important to you beyond the pain. Do you value connection, physical health, creativity, or self-care? Set goals that mirror these beliefs, adding meaning and purpose to your activities.

Start Small and precise: Aim for objectives that are precise, measurable, attainable, relevant, and time-bound (SMART). Instead of "get more exercise," strive for "walk for 15 minutes three times this week."

Focus on Action, Not simply Outcome: Don't simply create objectives for obtaining particular results, but also set goals for specific activities you can do each day. This keeps you focused on the journey, not simply the destination.

Celebrating Your Wins:
Acknowledge Your Efforts: Recognize the hard effort and bravery it takes to take even little steps ahead. Be pleased with yourself for every objective attained, no matter how seemingly trivial.

Reward Yourself: Celebrate your accomplishment with something you like, whether it's a soothing bath, a phone call with a loved one, or a delectable treat.

Share Your Successes: Talking about your triumphs with supportive friends or family may increase your excitement and build your support system.

Remember:
Be Patient and Flexible: There will be setbacks. Don't be disheartened; alter your goals as required and keep pushing forward.

Focus on the Journey: Enjoy the tiny moments of delight and satisfaction along the route. Healing is not a linear process; celebrate every success, large or little.

Seek Support: Don't hesitate to call out for help from experts, support groups, or loved ones. You are not alone on this path.

By setting little objectives and celebrating your accomplishments, you grow resilience, gain confidence, and find meaning despite the agony. Remember, every stride forward is a testimonial to your strength and a light of hope on your journey towards healing.

Finding Significance in the Midst of Loss: Creating Purpose from Pain

Grief can feel paralyzing, yet among the sorrow, individuals frequently discover an unexpected strength and determination to find meaning in their loss. This meaning can take various forms, offering comfort, purpose, and a sense of connection to your loved one's memories.

Exploring Avenues of Meaning:

Honoring Their Memory:
Engage in things your loved one enjoyed, keeping their spirit alive.

Create a scholarship or foundation in their honor to promote subjects they were passionate about.

Plant a memorial tree or garden in their honor.

Share their tale with others, keeping their memory fresh.

Helping Others:

Volunteer your time to groups relating to the cause of their death or their hobbies.

Offer assistance to individuals who are mourning, offering your experience and empathy.

Mentor or advise those facing similar issues your loved one overcome.

Personal Growth:
Pursue new talents or interests that your loved one motivated you to pursue.
Travel to locations they dreamed of seeing, experiencing the world through their eyes.

Focus on personal growth and self-discovery, recognizing their conviction in your potential.

Creative Expression:
Write poems, tales, or songs that capture your feelings and recollections.

Create art, music, or photography that embodies your loved one's spirit.

Participate in expressive therapies like dance or movement to process your sorrow in a creative way.

Finding What Resonates:
Be authentic: There's no "right" way to discover purpose. Choose activities that seem authentic and link you to your loved one in a unique way.

Start small: Don't feel forced to embark on extravagant gestures. Begin with basic tasks that bring warmth and a feeling of purpose.

Be patient: Finding significance requires time and research. Experiment with several alternatives and let yourself discover what resonates with you.

The Power of Purpose:
Engaging in activities that commemorate your loved one's memory, serve others, or foster personal growth can bring various benefits:

Reduced loneliness: Connecting with people via shared experiences or volunteering develops a sense of belonging and lowers feelings of loneliness.

Empowerment: Taking action enables you to convert your sadness into something constructive, establishing a sense of control and purpose.

Recovery: Focusing on helping others or personal improvement can provide a good diversion from your own sorrow and aid to your recovery path.

Honoring Their Legacy: Continuing their ideals, interests, or dreams via your actions keeps their memory alive and helps them to continue affecting the world in a meaningful way.
Remember:
Finding meaning is not about forgetting your loved one; it's about integrating your loss into your life in a way that honors their memory and helps you to go ahead with strength and purpose.

Every stride you take, large or small, is a monument to your perseverance and a celebration of your loved one's life.

Don't be hesitant to seek help from therapists, support groups, or loved ones while you traverse this road.

By exploring paths of meaning, you may convert your grief into a force for good, honoring your loved one's memory while paving the road for your own healing and progress.

Remember, you are not alone in your path through sorrow. Many others understand your difficulty and are here to help you. Reach out for support, connect with others, and allow yourself to recover. With time and assistance, you will find your way through the darkness and discover hope for the future.

Additional Resources:
Books:

"Healing Your Grieving Heart: 100 Practical Ideas for Adults and Teens" by Alan D. Wolfelt

"Whistling Vivaldi: How a Songbird Helped Me Learn to Grieve" by Claude Aubry

"Marley & Me: Life and Love with the World's Worst Dog" by John Grogan (For dealing with pet loss)

Healing After Loss: Daily Meditations for Working
Through Grief by Martha Whitmore Hickman

It's Okay That You're Not Okay: Meeting Grief
and Loss in a Culture That Doesn't Understand by
Megan Devine

The Year of Magical Thinking by Joan Didion
On Grief and Grieving: Finding the Meaning of
Grief Through the Five Stages of Loss by
Elisabeth Kübler-Ross and David Kessler

Holding On Letting Go: Finding Peace &
Forgiveness in Grief & Loss by Christopher Earle

Finding Meaning: The Sixth Stage of Grief by
David Kessler

Websites:
The National Center for Grieving Children &
Families

The Dougy Center: [https://www.dougy.org/]

The Compassionate Friends:
[https://www.compassionatefriends.org/]

The National Suicide Prevention Lifeline: 988

The Crisis Text Line: Text HOME to 741741

These are just a handful of the numerous tools available to help you cope with sorrow and loss. If you are feeling overwhelmed, please don't hesitate to call out for support. You are not alone.

Conclusion:

Whispers of Comfort: A Conclusion of Hope and Resilience

As we finish this book, remember, "Whispers of Comfort" were never meant to be a definitive guide, but a companion on your particular walk through loss. The trip is yours, and though the route may be long and twisting, you are not alone.

Within these pages, you've studied the nature of sorrow, its ups and downs, the force of hope, and the strength found in community. We've supplied practical tools, lit flames of hope, and offered a hand of support.

Now, when you flip the final page, remember this:

You are stronger than you realize. Grief may have knocked you down, but it cannot break you. Deep within you sits a reservoir of resilience, ready to be tapped. With each stride you take, with each tear you shed, you are getting stronger, more adaptive, more capable of navigating life's storms.

Hope is not a destination, but a journey. It does not guarantee the absence of pain, but the fortitude to carry it. Embrace the moments of delight, the laughing that bursts through the tears, the small sparks of light that lighten the gloom. These are the coals that will ignite your trip forward.

Community is your anchor. You are not alone in your pain. Reach out to loved ones, seek professional assistance, join online forums - connect with people who understand your path. Sharing your grief may be a source of enormous strength and comfort

Remember the whispers you've heard inside these pages:

Healing takes time. Be gentle with yourself, acknowledge your emotions, and allow yourself to mourn in your own manner. Memories are treasures. Cherish them, hold them near, and let them be a source of comfort and inspiration. New beginnings are conceivable. While the past cannot be reversed, the future brings the promise of pleasure, laughter, and love. Embrace new experiences and build new memories that memorialize your loved one and enrich your own life.

As you move on, bring these whispers with you. Let them be a gentle reminder of your power, your perseverance, and your potential to heal. The route ahead may be tough, but with optimism as your compass and community by your side, you will find your way.

As we finish this book, remember again that "Whispers of Comfort" are not meant to be a magic wand, but a shared lamp illuminating the journey through mourning. This journey may twist and turn, but know this: you are not alone, no matter your age or stage in life.

To our youngest readers: Even the tiny firefly may light a starless night. Though you might feel little right now, remember the strength and brightness you possess inside. Let that light radiate through your tears, your smiles, and your paintings. Share your whispers of comfort with loved ones, like sharing your favorite photo or cuddling together for a tale. Remember, even the tiniest gestures of kindness may provide consolation.

To our teens: Maybe right now, your world feels like a fractured mirror, reflecting shattered bits of what was. But remember, even fissures may become gateways to fresh development. Scars, though they depict the anguish, also indicate healing and perseverance. Use your voice to tell your tale, whether in a diary, online forum, or with a trusted friend. Your bravery inspires others, and sharing may ease the strain. Remember, you are stronger than you believe.

To our young adults: Navigating loss could feel like sailing through fog, unsure of the destination. But even amid the mist, the sun still beams, directing you towards a new horizon. Embrace the voyage, including the diversions and storms. Discover new talents, explore new routes, and remember, you are not defined by your loss. Share your whispers of comfort by providing help to others, volunteering, or following a hobby. Remember, you are worthy of experiencing joy again.

Imagine a glittering kaleidoscope, each piece expressing a distinct experience of sadness. Children, teenagers, young adults — we've all gone through its darkness and witnessed its dispersed light. Remember, this path isn't the same for everyone, yet inside each piece is a whisper of hope.

For the littlest stars:
Quote: "Even the smallest firefly can light up the darkest night." - Unknown

Message: You could feel little, lost, like a firefly in a storm. But remember, your light shines bright! Draw a picture of something pleasant and share it with someone you love. Together, we can fight away the darkness.

For the flowering sunflowers:
Quote: "The wound is the place where the Light enters you." - Rumi

Message: Life throws curveballs, and sadness may feel like a deep wound. But just like a sunflower moves towards the sun, remember your strength will develop. Share a word of hope with someone else hurting — you never know how much your light counts.

For the flying eagles:
Quote: "Sometimes you have to lose yourself to find yourself." - Anonymous

Message: This voyage could feel like soaring through fog, wondering where to land. But remember, even on dreary days, the sky contains unlimited potential. Explore new pathways, discover hidden strengths, and find your own unique wings. Share your tale with others — you'll discover you're not alone in this wide sky.

Remember, no matter your age, grief's whispers might sound different:

Children: Tears could flow freely, laughing comes in spurts. Embrace both, dear ones, for they're part of healing.

Teens: The world may appear unclear, emotions run high. Find safe locations to express yourself, and know you're not alone in the craziness.

Young Adults: The future can feel unknown, but you have the strength to build your own path. Embrace fresh beginnings, appreciate your loved ones, and remember that you are capable of wonderful things.

Quote: "The sun always rises after the darkest night." - Victor Hugo

As we complete our trip together, remember that grieving is not a destination, but a route we tread. It may be long and winding, filled with darkness and sorrow, but it is also paved with moments of brightness and resilience. Like the proverb above tells us, even in the darkest of nights, the sun will rise again, bringing with it the promise of a new dawn.

Carry this message of optimism and resilience with you. Share your whispers of comfort with others who are mourning, whether by a kind word, a listening ear, or just by being present. Remember, you are not alone on this path.

Go out, dear reader, with the whispers of comfort resonating in your heart. May your road be filled with light, love, and the strength to keep on.

Always remember:

You are adored.
You are strong.
You are not alone.

www.ingramcontent.com/pod-product-compliance
Lightning Source LLC
Chambersburg PA
CBHW050801260726
48660CB00004B/1184

9798880150779